PRAISE FOR LEW-ELLYN'S COLUMN

# Away with Words

*Ms. Hughes entertains her readers with a rich view of life's everyday experiences and relationships with children, family, and friends. With a quick wit and wonderful sense of humor, the author delights us with her stories— some humorous, others quite sobering—that bring us back to reality.*
   —JUDIE BAYLES, satisfied reader, Eustis, Maine

*Anything Lew-Ellyn writes is worth reading! She always makes me think… and smile!*
   —C.J. WORTHLEY, satisfied reader, Phillips, Maine

*An eloquent wordsmith.*
   —JAMIE VOSE, satisfied reader, Scarborough, Maine

# MAINE STORIES

From the writer
of the column
*Away with Words*

## LEW-ELLYN HUGHES

*Maine Stories*

©2016 Lew-Ellyn Hughes

ISBN: 978-1-940244-83-9

*designed and produced by*
Maine Authors Publishing
12 Hight Street, Thomaston, Maine
www.maineauthorspublishing.com


Printed in the United States of America

*To the staff at the Charles Shaw Library in Greenville, Maine:*
*I am forever grateful for your help and expertise.*

*And to Kay:*
*Thanks you very much for being the worlds' best proof reader.*
*What wood I had done without you?*

# CONTENTS

# CONTENTS

# MAINE
# STORIES

# INTRODUCTION

## *Sad Things*

EMILY WAS THE DAUGHTER WHO WANTED TOYS LIKE TRUCKS AND tools, and pets like salamanders and snakes. She never wore a dress, hardly ever washed her face, couldn't be bothered to come inside to pee, and refused to comb her hair so it stuck out in wild disarray, like she did—my wild child.

The summer she was three years old, Emily could be found on a mound of dirt in front of the house; it was her favorite place to play. The mound was supposed to be part of the lawn, but leveling it meant removing her mountain of imagination and I didn't have the heart to flatten her world by spreading and seeding mine. So there it remained: a mound of dirt with a grubby child perched atop, amid shovels and buckets, Matchbox cars and Tonka trucks. She was mistress of her mound where she played the day away.

Then one day, dishes joined the heap. Not just any dishes, but the child-size Tupperware set that belonged to her older sister, Kelly. The set was Kelly's prized possession, and Kelly kept them clean and neatly stacked next to her Easy-Bake Oven, ready to serve up wonderfully sweet little-girl treats. There they were: Kelly's dishes, in Emily's dirt pile. I quickly disentangled them from Emily's grimy little hands with an explanation that these dishes were for inside only, intended for sugar and spice and other things nice, not mud pies and chocolate worm cakes.

Emily, now the Empress of Indignation, had been woefully wronged, and she sat up there on her dirt pile the entire morning like a little wild mushroom, head bent, arms crossed, complaining to her crusty toes and rusty trucks, "It's a sad thing: a girl with no dishes."

For years after Emily's lament, my family, whenever disappointed or saddened, would use that phrase: "It's a sad thing: a girl with no dishes."

It's now over thirty years later, but I still haven't deciphered the message of a girl with no dishes, although I'm convinced there is one. Is it about growth? Is it about change? Is it that all little girls should have their heart's desire? Perhaps it's about learning to deal with disappointment. Maybe it's simply a story that says there will always be sad things, even for little girls. It's possible that there are several messages and the lesson is different for everyone. It's possible there is no message at all.

But I believe the message of Emily on her dirt pile teaches that all little girls, all women, no matter what their mound is made of or where they want to play, should still be allowed a nice set of dishes.

PART ONE

*Maine:*
*You Can't Get Here by Accident*

# Small-Town Maine

I LIVE IN A SMALL RURAL MAINE TOWN. EVERYBODY HERE KNOWS everybody else's truck and kids. We even know each other's pets. The other day my neighbor gave me a friendly chiding about my dog. "Your dog was in the road," he said. "If I'd been an eighteen-wheeler, he'd be a pancake."

"Talking about loose animals," I countered, "wasn't that your cow running around downtown last week?"

There is nothing like life in a small town. The big cities might hold all the powers, but Superman lived in Smallville, and the most powerful superglue to a community is how folks care for one another. We do that here. Big towns have community suppers for their hurting and needy and so do we, but we take it a step further and take up collections for our pets—like the time the dog that lives across the road didn't make it across the road and needed surgery to repair a broken leg. Coin collection cans showed up at all the cash registers in town for the pup.

At the local market, you'll find out who is ill or injured, who has suffered a death in the family, or who has been blessed by a birth. The caring folks over there will have a card for you to sign for that particular someone at the checkout—be it for comfort, condolences, or congratulations. (The new folks in town sign the card even if they don't know the recipient because it is highly likely the recipient knows them.)

The owners and staff at the market know your name and whether or not you want pickles on your tuna wrap. There's a chance, if you time it just right, when the manager Katie is getting deli innovative, you might be able to name the sandwich of the week—she let me name the Radical Roast Beef.

The aisles are full of specials—like friends and neighbors. We talk about important town issues, but also about muffin tops and back fat—not necessarily the things found on the shelves, but those horrible features found on our bodies after too many years of muffins and fatback. We stand at the meat counter, chatting about vegetables, gardening, the price of apples, and our priceless life here in the Western Maine mountains.

Another place to get the latest is at the post office, where I heard this conversation between two townsfolk:

"I see big changes at your place these days, Fred," Joe said.

"How so?" asked Fred.

"I see you and the missus have switched parking spots in your driveway."

We enjoy small-community immunity from big-town woes like distrust. Here, the folks at the local gas station know me so they don't make me prepay (of course, they also know where I live).

Just like big towns, our town has it all: cross-dressers and cross bearers, businessmen and busybodies, rich and poor, young and old, eccentric and boring, famous and infamous…but we have only one or two (or a few) of each and we know them by name. That makes us a collection, a cooperative, a community—a small Maine town.

# *True Mainers?*

I MET A MAN, AN ARTIST WHO LIVES OFF THE MAIN ROAD, DEEP IN THE woods, past all the mailboxes. He's an internationally known potter, famous for his beautiful, wood-fired creations.

"Where are you from?" I asked him during our get-to-know-each-other conversation.

"I'm not from anywhere," he replied. And because he spoke like an artist, I thought, "Oh, it's the free-spirited side of him answering. He's going to say something like, 'I am from the earth; I am from the soil, like my clay…'"

But no, he clarified himself with a rather bland, disappointing explanation. "I'm not from anywhere because I was brought up in the military."

"I was brought up in the military, and I'm from somewhere!" I said, and then continued, "Your family is from somewhere, and we are from our families. Come on, man, where are you from?"

"Pennsylvania," he humbly answered.

\* \* \*

Near the summit of a nearby mountain, I stopped to rest a bit and exchanged pleasantries with a couple who were doing the same.

"Pretty rugged hike, huh?" I asked.

"Yes, especially when you have to cross those cricks," the man answered.

I asked him where he was from.

"Maine," he smiled.

"No, you're not," I braved.

"Yes I am; I'm from York," he insisted.

"I don't think anyone from Maine, even from York, pronounces *creek* as *crick.*"

His smile cracked. He lowered his gaze and admitted, "I'm from Georgia."

* * *

I was forced to watch her; she was in my way. I could see bits and pieces of her through her window, through my window. She wore copper bangle bracelets and age spots on her arm and a huge silver plastic heart pendent around her neck that matched her hair color. It banged against the steering wheel as she maneuvered her car into its place.

She was a dolled-up old doll. She slowly,

carefully,

slowly,

slow…

…ly

ever

so

slow…

…ly backed into the parking space beside mine so as not to cause any more damage to her rusting Chevy Impala—its lines of corrosion partially hidden under pink-and-black zebra-print duct tape—there, and over there, and over that spot and there, too.

A dolled-up old doll driving a dolled-up old doll.

She IS a Mainer. I could tell.

# A Dying Breed

It has become my habit to stop into a mom-and-pop store halfway between Stratton and Greenville for a cup of coffee. The old guys who gather for their morning coffee at this local market are my kind of coffee mates. They hang around the counter, one hand tucked into the front pocket of their jeans, one knee cocked. I think that position is what keeps them from toppling forward; they are so bent from age and hard-won life victories. The other hand is wrapped around a paper cup of the steaming brew as they discuss whatever needs discussing that particular day. I listen to the thoughts and opinions they share. They speak with wisdom that only experience teaches.

I think many folks these days could learn a lot from them.

I suppose these men get up in the morning and meet at the local market because all their lives they got up in the morning and left their homes to go do something productive. They went to the fields, the mill, the shop, or to the log or construction truck. It's what they always did so they continue, out of habit or conviction, to get up in the morning and get going. Because they provide one another with conversation and companionship, they remain productive.

Again, I think many folks these days could learn a lot from their example.

"Well, here's the old goat," said one as another entered, the door and his bones creaking as he limped his way in.

The old hen behind the counter defended this new arrival. "Well, if that ain't the pot callin' the kettle black!" she cackled.

The first time I happened upon this place and this group, I was floundering around the offerings at the coffee counter. I didn't know where anything was. I put my cup of coffee under what I thought was the creamer button.

"Nope," drawled one. "I think you'll find that to be hot chocolate." His speech was as slow as his smile as he watched me realize my near blunder.

I reached for a plastic cover.

"Nope," repeated another. I looked at him. "In the back." He smiled and pointed his chin toward the correct pile of tops. (I began to suspect I was the morning entertainment.)

One gentleman stood tall over the magazine rack (and most certainly head and shoulders above the Hollywood beauties who adorn those pages). His face was deeply lined. I call those story lines. I would later find his stories to be fascinating in their ordinary uniqueness.

These guys graciously let me spend a few moments with them, probably because I remarked that being watched by good-looking men was making me nervous and that's the reason I almost put hot chocolate in my coffee instead of creamer. Whenever we gather, I sip and stay mostly silent, savoring their conversation, their views, their bantering, the twinkle in their eyes, and every moment.

I love Maine back roads, mom-and-pop stores, and rich characters, so I enjoy them as often as I am able.

# Mama's Whistle

IT WAS SIX AGAINST ONE. BUT THAT ONE WAS IN CONTROL BECAUSE SHE had a whistle. When Mama stood (all four feet, eleven inches of her) on the front porch and that shrill sound resonated through the woods around our summer camp on Moosehead Lake, the six came running.

The littlest sister appeared from under the blueberry bushes down front, and another sister grabbed the limb of a sturdy birch tree and with a Tarzan-like swing leaped from the top of our huge climbing rock out back. The middle child stopped digging in the worm pit down the well path, the family bookworm put his reading down, and I scrambled over the rocks that lined the shore. The youngest child tried to join us, but he was tethered by a safety harness to the pine tree in the front yard, and he ran in place with his effort.

We were trained to come running immediately when we heard her call, because like little rats in a Skinner box, we were conditioned to believe the whistle meant something good: food usually, but sometimes it meant company had arrived or we were going to town, to Greenville. Occasionally that meant a trip to Harris Drugstore Dairy Bar for an ice-cream cone. Being soft-serve ice milk, the ice cream wasn't pure, but the bliss we experienced eating it certainly was.

It must have been a challenge to keep track of six little kids who had been set free from the confines of the classroom for the summer. Mama had too many kids to call, so she whistled.

Those days of summer were carefree times, full of the fun of childhood. We were free as birds and wild as the critters that called our woods home. There were so many things to do and so much to discover. Our play was boundless thanks to the vastness of our imaginations, and I believe we grew up before our creativity ran dry.

I remember checking pinecones for seeds. That became my childhood challenge—to not leave one fallen cone untouched in the search of one tiny seed left behind by a chipmunk or squirrel, but they were thorough little beasts and I never found any.

I collected rocks from the water's edge, each one unique and beautiful—like snowflakes (though rock collections last longer). If we found a rock with a ring of quartz embedded all the way around it, it was deemed special and we would make a wish and throw it into the lake. I'm pretty sure all my childhood wishes came true. Many days I never donned a shoe, and my bathing suit was my outfit of choice.

We splashed, we climbed, we jumped, we ran. We swung in the hammock or from the tree branches—always within earshot of Mama's whistle, and we never failed to come running when we heard it.

As I write this I can hear the robins and chickadees in the backyard chirping wildly. I glance up from my desk to watch the birds and notice the road into town lined with cars—kayaks and canoes on top, campers in tow. It's the summer folk arriving and ready to play.

I hear the sound of the birds again, whistling their morning song. Mama has too many kids to call, so she whistles.

And the children come running.

# Vacationland

I OWN TWO PAIRS OF FALL HIKING BOOTS, FOUR PAIRS OF SNOW BOOTS, A pair of cross-country ski boots, three pairs of alpine ski boots, a pair of snowmobile boots, six pairs of sneakers, and more sets of comfy summer sandals (and not so comfy high heels) than I care to admit. The one thing my footwear collection lacks is mud boots because it's during mud season that I take my spring runoff. I leave as soon as the snow does.

The only detail of this year's trip that remains undecided is where I should go. I'm tempted to go to the ocean. It doesn't cost a thing to sit by the sea and dream. I love the sea almost as much as I love these mountains where my home is nestled. The coast is clear of snow by mid-April, isn't it?

Perhaps I'll go to "The County"—that's where my ancestors lived, labored, and loved. I could go back to my beginnings. Besides, it's quiet and peaceful up there and the Aroostook County farmlands—with their barns and fields—are soothingly picturesque, like the coast is delightfully scenic, like the mountains are breathtakingly beautiful.

Perhaps I should go east—Downeast. I love how they speak down there. It's like a different world, yet it's not, it's still Maine.

I know! I'll go to the islands. (I have several friends on several.) I find their way of life invigorating (and delicious), so unlike life anywhere else, and yet it's not anywhere else, it's here.

Maybe it would be best if I went home to Greenville and Moosehead Lake. Mama would like that, and a visit with her always makes good fodder for wacky stories.

I realize some of the places I've mentioned are also covered in mud this time of year, but strangely enough, I don't mind looking at someone else's mud. Maybe I'll go to all those places. Heaven knows, Maine's mud season can certainly last long enough for me to visit each, and we do have them all: islands, lakes, mountains, farms, and fields. I'll figure it out. There is one thing for sure: I won't leave Maine for my vacation. I don't need to.

## Pitch and Pinking Shears

EVERY MAINE KID HAS AT ONE TIME OR ANOTHER POKED A SPRUCE TREE. Popping sap bubbles was one of our favorite things to do as kids summering on Moosehead Lake. Armed with a good sharp stick, I would seek the juiciest sap sacks and stab the day away. Every once in a while I would hit a good one: a bubble of sap that, when punctured, didn't bleed down the bark, but pitched a revengeful fit and hit me square in the face. It tasted nasty, and I wondered how the Native Americans got past the "spit-it-out" stage when they chewed spruce gum. (I also wondered if popping sap bubbles was how they discovered that gum.)

Since Mama considered it too much work to wash play clothes for six children who played outside from dawn to dusk, we wore bathing suits from June to September. A bathing suit wardrobe was her answer to the problem of an ever-growing laundry pile from her ever-growing family. We wore our suits all day and hung them on the line each night to dry and air out for the next morning. Skimpy suits, sap sacks, and sharp sticks being what they were and physics being what it was, the airborne pitch often ended up on our skin. We put sand on the sticky spot and rubbed vigorously until the pitch and quite a few layers of skin were removed. I remember having several untanned scrub marks on my neck, arms, and legs.

The ultimate bad luck of poking a spruce tree were those especially regrettable days when the pitch landed in my hair. Sometimes the tree's counterattack would happen so fast I wasn't aware that I had been spewed on until much later. When I had tired of stabbing trees, I would play in the woods or at the beach where my glob of hairborne pitch would acquire sand, tiny pebbles, ladybugs, pine needles, or other bits of forest floor. I would walk around ignorant that I had a pitchy clump of stuff cemented to the top of my head. I recall one time my sister's hair sap glob picked up a tiny piece of spruce bough and a lightening bug; she looked as if she had a miniature Christmas tree on her head, complete with a blinking light.

Modern moms use peanut butter to save the day and the do; my mother used pinking shears—those sewing scissors with notched blades that leave a zigzag design in whatever they cut. For those of you who had normal mothers and boring childhoods, I'll explain. With six kids and a dog, my mother didn't have time for fancy (and by fancy, I mean even) haircuts. Mama would haul out the kitchen stool, place the pathetically pitched kid upon it, and yell, "Bring me the pinking shears!" Because in the end—and for the ends—pinking shears cover a thousand sins.

They say we are a product of our childhood, which would explain my present-day jagged edges and choppy endings.

## *Quiet Stillness*

THERE IS SUCH A QUIET STILLNESS ON THESE ICY WINTER MORNINGS.

It seems that one small noise—even one tiny mouse movement—would be the bomb blast that shatters this frozen morning sky and the entire day would fall.

I rose early to get a few things accomplished—things that would clatter and bang.

The silence won't allow it.

Instead of noise disturbing the quiet, it's the quiet that rules this morning.

# General Store Gingerbread

THERE'S A TINY GENERAL STORE ON A TINY ISLAND OFF THE COAST OF Maine. I suppose there are lots of tiny stores on Maine's tiny islands, but I happened to land in this particular one. This little store is also the island's post office and restaurant as well as its coffee and antique shop. When I entered, the store was occupied only by the postmistress and a woman behind the counter who was most likely the restaurant's lone waitress and the store's cashier—I never did find out for certain.

"It's nice and quiet in here," I remarked as I sat down at the counter. (I was just making conversation, as it was nice and quiet everywhere on the tiny island.)

"Yes, it is," she agreed, then paused and added, "for a few minutes, before the rush."

I could not imagine a rush of folks (or folks in a rush) down here, and I thought she was joking. I chuckled.

"Really," she insisted. "The gingerbread is almost out of the oven; this place is about to get very busy."

"People come every day for gingerbread?" I asked.

"Everyone knows when it's baked, and everyone is going to show up."

"The entire island?" I was skeptical.

"*Everyone.*" She spoke very slowly.

"It must be darn good gingerbread," I said.

"Well, the funny thing is, it's not really gingerbread. As a matter of fact, there's no ginger in it at all."

The door opened and, as the first gingerbread-seekers entered, she headed to the cash register and said over her shoulder, "It's a white cake made with nutmeg."

The gingerbread people formed a line behind the cash register and paid for the delicacy before it had even arrived from the kitchen. Then they stood around and waited as more gingerbread men and women showed up—and they did. The store filled up in a snap.

And then the gingerbread that wasn't really gingerbread showed up. Sure enough, arriving in the hot-mitted little hands of the baker were two pans of white cake—just like the cake my grandmother used to make for everyone's birthday—plain old white cake, sans icing.

The baker placed the hot pans gingerly on the counter.

I looked at the pans, and then looked at the crowd of people. I was thinking how they might live for this gingerbread (that wasn't), but I live for this sort of story. Camera in hand, I approached the counter and snapped a picture of the cakes.

A gentleman sitting nearby noticed and asked me, "Are you a reporter?"

"No," I said, "I'm just amazed."

So amazed, in fact, that I didn't have the presence of mind to find out why this white cake became known on this island as gingerbread or even how it tasted. I was so busy being amazed and watching people that the treat sold out before I could decide whether or not I wanted a piece. I had never been a fan of gingerbread, but this gingerless concoction was an entirely different story, and I was disappointed that it was gone so soon. It was consumed faster than the time it took to cook it, faster than the time it took me to tell you about it, faster than the ferry that brought me to it, and much, much faster than my mind, because I did not think to ask how this obviously delicious but observably white cake became known to islanders as gingerbread. It was gone in a flash, then too were the folks who loved it.

A not-so-gentle tug on my arm reminded me that the ferry back to the mainland would also be gone in a flash, so my curiosities were like the folks who didn't make it to the store: unsatisfied.

# The Road

I LOVE A ROAD TRIP. I DON'T GET TO GO OFTEN, BUT WHEN I DO, MY journeys are lengthy and scenic, mostly because I have the world's worst sense of direction. Seriously, it's a triumph that I know which way is up the stairs.

On one such divagation, my cell phone rang. It was my grandson calling.

"Hi, Grandmother, whatcha doin'?"

"I'm traveling," I answered.

"Where are you?"

"I'm not exactly sure," I said.

There was panic in his voice. "Well, for crying out loud, Grandmother, pull over!" (If you're lost, not sure of where you're going, pull over—good advice for road trips and life.) But I didn't. I have yet to pull over even when the journey takes me into unfamiliar, really scary territory, because somehow I always end up where I'm supposed to be (albeit often with frazzled nerves and sometimes a day late). Besides, the scenery is just too interesting to miss by quitting.

The upside to these accidental adventures is the sheer joy of witnessing the personality of the countryside. If the interstate is the businessman of travel—every mile serious, sterile, and boring—then Maine's back country roads are the hippies—free, fun, and full of individuality. Anything and everything goes on country roads, and it appears the first to go is correct spelling. Last fall, *pumpkin* seemed to be the target, and I've seen it spelled "pumken," "punkin," and "punken."

My all-time favorite misspelled country sign had boldly painted words that announced "redemption cenner." I think the guy on the coast who says he'll work for bottles and cans should consider opening his own redemption cenner. I'm not judging; I'm enjoying. I can't criticize others; there are times when my spelling is so poor, even my spell-checker shrugs.

On the back roads, I've seen Mainers at their most authentic: the homeowners who have a dead pickup truck parked out front, and even though it doesn't run (no tires was the first clue), it's still useful as a garbage truck—its body is full almost to spilling over of bagged-up household garbage. This amazes and puzzles me. All I can do is wonder.

The sight that still makes me scratch my head is the one I saw on a desolate road, way out in the boonies. There was a tractor parked at the end of a driveway. It had a love seat in its bucket, lifted high into the air. Short of stopping to ask why, I'll never understand the logic of lifting it. And as strange as that is, it gets wilder; there was a raccoon asleep on the cushions.

You just never know what you're going to see out there along Maine's byways, and sometimes you have to take your eyes off the road to appreciate it.

# Here She Comes

Here she comes. She's beautiful, she's cool, she's popular. She meets all the requirements to be head cheerleader. She's the pinup girl on the calendar. She's autumn.

My favorite thing about her is she doesn't bug me when I go outside.

Still, for all autumn's finer points, she has a chill about her: she forces us to button up our houses and our overcoats. She chases children indoors, into school buildings specifically, so not too many kiddos are enamored with her. Autumn's fan base is made up of mature people, those closer to the autumn of their lives (maybe because we appreciate her more).

I had always assumed autumn is called "fall" because of what the leaves do, but that's not why. It's because the sun seems to fall from the sky as it lowers closer to the horizon, stopping when it reaches the autumnal equinox. And with the sun goes summer; it literally falls away. The word *autumn* comes from the root word *autu-*, which has within it connotations of the passing of the year. That sounds a little melancholy, but there is a silver lining: in the old Irish language, *autumn* means "under winter." I like that. I like knowing that fall is still there, she's just hidden. After learning this, every time I see a brilliantly colored fallen leaf peeking out of the snow, I think to myself, "Ah, there she is—just under winter."

So, say good-bye to heat and humidity and say hello to pumpkins and sweaters, for here she comes. It's about time.

# Mouse War

THIS TIME OF YEAR, IT'S NOT UNCOMMON FOR MICE TO BUILD THEIR winter homes inside Maine homes, and recently one mouse decided that my house was good for him. My feelings on the subject: inside the barn, okay; inside the abandoned farmhouse up the road, fine; in my attic, no, absolutely not!

I set a trap with a slice of cheese. The next morning, the cheese was gone, but the trap remained intact.

Plan B was to use peanut butter. The sly mouse ate every lick again without setting off the trap. I checked the tension on the spring; it was sensitive. This was one smart mouse.

Still, I believed my IQ was higher.

I sprinkled oatmeal in all the prepositional places: around, in, under, on, and between the mechanisms of the mousetrap. Surely the mouse would set it off this time. Nope. Every stinking flake was consumed. I started to wonder if my IQ really was that much higher.

It was time to bring in reinforcements. I called the two young men who rent rooms in my home and asked them if they would take up arms against the intruder. They gladly accepted the challenge, wringing their hands in gleeful anticipation and telling stories about the traps their grandfathers built to outsmart smartened critters.

Their first trap involved an empty cocoa container lined with duct tape (sticky side up) with a hefty helping of peanut butter in it. Cardboard ramps led to a hole in the top. The boys hoped the mouse would take the trip up those ramps to its grave. The only thing the sticky tape did was give the mouse traction to escape with a belly full of peanut butter.

Their next plan involved a spinning dowel laden with peanut butter and strategically placed across the top of a water-filled compound bucket. When the mouse stepped on the dowel, it would spin, and the mouse would lose his footing and the war. Before this trap was completed, however, I found out something about our resident mouse that changed our course of action: to my horror I saw mouse droppings in my bathroom vanity drawer. I tore the vanity apart and disinfected the entire thing. When I pulled out the bottom drawer, I discovered that a package of Tylenol Cold & Flu tablets had been opened and chewed on; a fine white powder remained, and it covered the area. Mouse poop mixed in with the powder was evidence of the culprit.

Our mouse was a druggie.

I informed the troops of this discovery. All the fun war games needed to be put aside. We had no choice but to fight fire with fire. We resorted to something I don't like to do, something that goes against my belief system: chemical warfare. I donned some plastic gloves, a face mask, rubber boots, and a knee-length raincoat before opening a box of d-CON mouse poison and placing it in the attic. War over. Story over. Except…

I'll never be sure if I won this battle since there won't be any evidence of the victory. In the end, this mouse might have the last laugh if I happen upon his ugly carcass and the frightening sight startles me to death.

## *Local Flavor*

A FEW YEARS BACK, A LOCAL BAR OWNER TOLD ME THE STORY OF A WOMAN from England who stopped into his place of business during the height of hunting season for a toddy and a taste of local flavor. She made her way through the throng of hunters as she headed to a bar stool.

She and the bartender struck up a conversation; her English accent was the flag that declared she was "from away." After finding out she was from Europe, he asked if this was her first time in Maine. She told him it was her first time anywhere in the United States.

"How do you like it?" he asked.

"I think it's beautiful here, but I have a question," she said as she surveyed the crowded room of jolly hunters who were fresh out of the woods, still in their hunting attire. She turned back to the bartender and asked, "Why do you dress all your drunks in orange?"

They either don't have hunter-safety orange or drunks in Europe—I'm guessing it's orange.

# Lunch at a Diner

I'M HAVING LUNCH AT A 1950S DINER; HERE'S WHAT'S ON THE MENU.

The wall in the dining room boasts a mural of a 1950s-era movie theater advertising a showing of *The Bridge on the River Kwai* starring William Holden and Alec Guinness. All the cars in the mural parking lot are appropriately aged Chevys—beautiful pieces of art in art.

In keeping with the drive-in theme, a collection of Maine vanity license plates covers another wall and shows off the quirkiness of our state and our drivers: "MAINAH," "FAHMA," "FIFTY7," "GI-JOE."

Elvis and the Everly Brothers serenade the diners from the intercom, but this place feels so authentic, I want to check to see if they are in the next room.

The locals eat here, including one famous local in particular. I won't mention his name except to say he is considered the king of the horror story and this diner is in Bangor, Maine. He's not here today, but I know he has been. Although I don't read him because he scares me, I've eaten here with him on other occasions (of course our booths, like our genres, were far apart).

Here I sit, out of place, loving it and taking it all in while trying not to be noticed noticing the other diners. I have borrowed a pen from the waitress and am scribbling observances on the back of my paper placemat in between bites. (The front is full of advertisements.)

The old veterans, farmers, and lumbermen limp in and out. Their bodies are worn down, but their appetites are not, and the meatloaf dinner with mashed Maine potatoes from "The County" seems to be the hot-ticket item of the day.

There is a lady with clips in her long white hair. On one side are three clear plastic clasps, and on the other is a bobby pin, a simple brown clip, and one that is a whimsical green butterfly with wings at the ready, waiting for the breeze from a flip of her head to take flight.

I imagine her wild, thick locks needed all those clips for control during the celebrations after World War II; she must have been quite a dish! Today, I believe she wears them more for her heart than her thinning hair.

Two hunters walk past my table. One smiles and winks at me. He enters the booth opposite mine, sits lengthwise on the seat and watches me. A stalker?

There is an elderly lady with shoulder-length flamboyant orange earrings and a black eye. She's laughing with her friends; her earrings dance. My mind goes where the colors take it: she's either black and blue from living a life full of adventurous dancing or from fighting for the right to be herself and to wear those dangling orange creations.

The gentleman in front of me is huge. He has three rolls on the back of his neck—those fat rolls that are adorable and kissable on a baby are not so on a full-sized man. Unlike him, I'll decline the waitress's offer of a slice of Maine blueberry pie because I own a bakery and my occupation as "The Pie Lady" has stained my fingertips and my taste for that treat (not to mention how the rolls in front of me have been an influence).

Although I'm not finished (I could stay here all day), my turkey bacon wrap and the space on my placemat are gone.

So then, am I.

# Short Stories

A STORY DOESN'T HAVE TO BE LONG AND INVOLVED TO BE GOOD. I LOVE the magic found in few words and short stories. We all have favorites; these are a few of mine.

## A Fish Tale

My daughter Holland and her friends like to fish. On one fishing trip they netted a twenty-one-inch trout, but that wasn't the real catch. Upon cleaning the fish, they found five baby crayfish in its gut. Holland kept one as a pet and to keep it alive, she fed it bits of the trout.

I love stories of poetic justice. They leave me feeling well-fed and satisfied.

## Mrs. Curtis's Cupboard

Mrs. Curtis feared she would be forced to leave her valuables behind when she and her young son fled their Portland home as the Great Fire of 1866 roared around them. She placed many of her treasured household items in a cherished cupboard—as many as this fine piece could hold—and ran out into the street to hire a cart, a truck—anything—to carry her things to safety. The streets were in chaos. There were none to save her; they were all too busy trying to save themselves.

When she returned from her search, she saw looters had entered her home and were emerging with the cupboard. She silently followed the thieves as they carried her beloved piece away. When they reached a place far from the flames, she cried out to other fleeing citizens who came to her aid. The robbers abandoned the piece and ran, having delivered it and all it held to safety.

By far, my favorite stories are those that happen right in front of me as I am going about my day and my business. This one I overheard in a checkout line, and nothing out of Hollywood can match it. It was a conversation between old friends.

## *Two Old-Timers*

Two old-timers, who obviously knew each other, were standing in front of me. One of them was quite beat up; his face was black and blue, and his arm was in a sling. His leg was bandaged and lame so he held a cane to help him walk.

The other old-timer gave his injured friend the once-over, shook his head, and asked, "Good Lord in heaven, Harold, what'd ya do?"

"Fell off the barn roof," explained Harold.

"Lay there long?" his friend wanted to know.

"Nope. Mother came right quick and called them ambulance folks."

"How far'd ya fall?"

Harold thought for a moment. "'Bout twenty feet."

His friend sucked in his lips, nodded his head again, and said with same-experience empathy, "Twenty feet, huh? Goes quick, don't it?"

This is not the end, for great short stories should never end.

# Traveling Back in Time

As I hopped into my car this cold January morning and began driving, I started wondering how our ancestors managed to maneuver on winter roads, especially around central and northern Maine. I found out that travel back in my great-grandmother's time was actually easier in winter. During the warmer seasons, the roads were rutted, full of deep mud, and usually unusable. Winter roads were frozen and therefore more maneuverable. A popular mode of travel then was by pung—a horse-drawn box on runners. Every picture I can find of a pung shows an open sleigh with no top or sides to keep the weather out or the heat in (that had to be miserable!).

Summer travel could be just as uncomfortable. A tourist wrote about his 1853 trip by stagecoach and then by mud wagon (a lighter, smaller, and therefore faster wagon) from Waterville to Greenville. It took eighteen hours to travel those seventy-two miles. Part of the road they traveled was a washboard of unhewn logs, and as the writer explained, his attempt to entertain his fellow travelers by reciting Henry Wadsworth Longfellow's poem "Evangeline" went something like this: "Thihis ihis thehe fohorest prihihimeheval; thehe murhurmuring pihines hahand thehe hehemlohocks!" (That makes hitting our occasional pothole seem like just a mere bump in the road!)

These poor coach travelers were subject to lengthy delays between destinations due to impassable road conditions. They would become stranded at roadside inns for days (sometimes weeks), where they waited for the roads to freeze enough to keep the axles and horses' bellies above the mud. On the road, they suffered exposure to swarms of mosquitoes in the spring, choking dust in the summer, and bone-jolting rides year round. I've read so many stories of sleighs being upended and the riders being flung out into snowbanks or the coach becoming stuck in a fence that it makes our occasional turn in the snowbank seem like child's play.

Even with all their problems, wagons were the best way to get around. Greenville children would hitch a ride to school on the back of the milkman's wagon, dragging their feet in the snow the entire way, but thankful for the lift.

Eventually, travel by train replaced the stagecoach. My grandmother and her siblings took the Bangor and Aroostook railway from Greenville Jct. to Bangor to do such things as visit the dentist. It was an all-day affair and tiring, but because the mail returned with them in the evening, the village folk would be waiting at the station and it became a daily social event—something that weary travelers and townsfolk alike looked forward to.

In the 1940s, my mother took the "Scoot," a train that scooted from Greenville Jct. to Brownville Jct., to attend her high-school basketball games. "The roads," she explained, "if they existed at all, were so rough or in such a state of disrepair that going by train was really our only option. We would be gone almost all night! It was an adventure and we loved it," she added.

As history goes, my mother's childhood wasn't that long ago, but we've made leaps and bounds in the transportation department since then.

I wouldn't want to travel back in time. Traveling in these modern days, even during a snowstorm, although sticky or slippery at best, is pretty simple in comparison.

# This Old House

SHE STARTS HER PREDAWN GRUMBLING AROUND FOUR O'CLOCK ON THESE deeply cold winter mornings. At first she politely creaks, but I'm used to that, so I roll over and go back to sleep. She then bangs loudly to bring me fully aware that she wants attention. Her objective is to wake me up so I'll warm her up by feeding the household fires. She is old and cold, cranky and complaining, unwilling to wait any longer. It seems it's all about her, and as I drag myself out of bed, I find myself wondering if it's time for me to give her up and move on. She is a fortress that demands my time, money, and fortitude. But like any lady, she's worth it. And besides, she is something I've always wanted: an old farmhouse in the mountains. I have come to believe that in calling myself her owner, the joke is on me. The truth is it's quite the other way around. Because this is where I belong, and she owns me.

I think of all she has survived. She's been around for more than one hundred years and has passed the test of time. Even after all the interior changes by those who lived here before—old walls torn down, new ones added, new paint, refurbished rooms and roof—her foundation has never really changed. Her lines have settled in pleasant places, and she stands where she always stood because that is what she is meant to do. She is what she is: a sturdy home alongside an ever-changing brook in an inevitably ever-changing little town.

Families of old were born here, grew up here, and then left her. She doesn't mind, really. She recognizes that is the way of life. New families will always replace the old, and they will also walk her antique oak floors, passing the new portraits hung on her walls.

I wonder if she has a favorite family. Was it the one with five boys or the one with three girls? I somehow doubt she favors individuals, but I believe she's happy so long as there is contentment within the hearts of those who reside within.

She has sheltered many. She has been a safe haven for the fledgling, a refuge to the homeless, and a comfort to the weary traveler. She is the birthplace of solid friendships, and along the way has weathered rain inside and out. She is full of all those things that make a life full. So, I guess I'll keep her—splinters, chipping paint, leaks, and her clanking and complaining—for just a bit longer.

# Warm Thoughts on Winter

WE HAVE A SAYING HERE IN MAINE: "THERE'S NO SUCH THING AS BAD weather, only inappropriate clothing." But the recent morning temperature of −24 degrees is pushing that belief to the limit and making me wonder just how cold it can get out there. If I'm to believe the record books, Maine's coldest recorded temperature was −48 up in Van Buren back in 1925, meaning that we're only halfway there. Still, those one or two days of super subzero temperatures makes me appreciate the teens; after twenty-four below, sixteen above feels like a heat wave.

Mother Nature is a cold-hearted, stubborn woman and will have her way, but we have our ways of keeping warm as she tries to freeze us out (of state). We chop kindling, lug armloads of firewood or bags of pellets, shovel snow from the walk and driveways, rake it off the roofs, and when we are finished, we do the same for our neighbors who cannot.

Such work keeps us warm; doing it for ourselves warms us outwardly, doing it for others warms us inwardly.

Mainers have learned to take the cold in stride. When asked by a southerner how he stands the northern icy temperatures, an old-timer (some say it was Greenville's elderly Doc Pritham) replied, "We don't stand, and we don't sit, either—we keep moving!" That's what we need to do: keep moving, keep moving forward like the calendar, and eventually those hot, humid, energy-zapping days of July will return. Remember those dog days when all we could do was hang out on our porches, panting and praying for a breeze? Those days when you couldn't get away from your own sweat no matter where you went? And even though I probably complain about winter just as much as the next guy, I prefer it over those oppressive, breathless days.

You can breathe in winter. Winter is beautiful. Winter air is fresh, it's crystal, and clearly for a lot of us, it's a huge part of our livelihood here in the western Maine mountains. I've said it before: like my donuts, I prefer my mountains sugared. I guess that makes me a snow-flake. Plus, I'd rather be bitten by a chill than a mosquito any day!

I understand why people think those of us who love winter are tilted off our axis. It's because we are. Besides, we can't all live in the south; who would make maple syrup and snowmen?

So why do we stay here? Some say it's because Mother Nature is not the only stubborn thing in Maine. But those of us who know, know it's because it's home.

# It's Over

IT'S OVER. IT TRULY IS. AS I LIE IN BED IN THE LIGHT OF DAWN, THE QUIET that surrounds me is so alarming it wakes me up. I am startled. My eyelids flutter open, and I look from left to right and back again as if I am being tricked. There must be sound somewhere! I listen and after a moment, I understand. The absolute silence confirms it—the end has indeed come. The silence says it all: the oil furnace isn't running. Winter has ended.

Then I have a second thought. "Perhaps it's the furnace, not winter, that's died. And if that's the case, it must be from exhaustion!" On my way to the basement to investigate, I open the kitchen door to allow the dog out, and I feel it immediately. The northern Maine air no longer stings—it's mild. It's actually pleasant!

I breathe a sigh of relief. The furnace and I have made it through another winter. This season was a tough one—it was cold; it was lengthy. But we proved tougher with heartier endurance than a very strong-willed, cold-hearted Mother Nature.

This morning's skies are dark, but my home is made bright by a lamp lit, a hot cup of coffee, and the sweet sound of rain on the roof. Rain is a sure sign of spring and will wash away the old and the cold, making the way clean and clear for the new.

This year I saw some things I have never seen before.

I saw a chipmunk coming out of a hole in the snow. It must have been the entrance to his nest. I thought that I must have looked just like that to the heavenlies as I emerged from my home after this year's many heavy snowstorms.

I saw a crow choose a particular twig from a tree, snap it off, and fly away with it, presumably to build her nest. That was a new sight for me. I thought birds only used twigs and things lying on the ground.

That's my favorite thing about spring—it's a promise of new. And now, here comes a fresh one after thousands of springs gone by.

She comes, bearing the same old newness: new growth, new life full of brand new promises…there will even be new old stuff showing up at the dump.

My favorite thing about spring is it's about the new. This year I discovered that even after decades of springs, new discoveries can still be made.

# Wild Animal Encounters

I NEARLY RAN INTO A MOOSE BUTT. I WAS MOUNTAIN BIKING ON A DIRT road, when all of a sudden the beast exited the forest on my right and ran down the road in front of me. His massive rear end was just a few inches from my front end! I didn't stop peddling, I didn't even slow down; I enjoyed every stinking minute as I thought, "How cool is this?"

Then there was the time I was hiking in the woods near my home and a coyote trotted past alongside me. I thought it odd that this deer-killing wild dog would come that close and not give me a second glance, but it didn't occur to me to turn and run. I thought, "Wow! That was amazing!"

I was telling these wilderness animal stories to a group of young adults who were visiting from Europe. They listened with awe and amazement as I explained nonchalantly that it is inevitable to experience wildlife encounters here in the northern Maine woods.

I told them of the time I was snowshoeing on Snow Mountain when I came across two sets of animal prints. One was obviously from a deer, and the second set was that of a cat—a big cat—whose paw was larger than my palm. I remember thinking, "As long as that cat follows that deer, I'm probably safe." I did not consider aborting my plan to reach the top, so I continued my trek.

I told them about the day I came across a bridge and met a mother moose with her baby. The baby's leg was temporarily caught between the wooden planks of the bridge, and the mommy moose seemed to turn into a mother bear as she snorted at me to BACK OFF until her young'un could get free. I did; not with fear, but with respect and fascination.

I told them of the time I tiptoed behind a bobcat so I could watch his beautifully colored form saunter along, and the time I watched a baby moose stand up for the first time after its birth. I spoke of how I watched a mother and baby bear scratch at the fallen leaves of autumn to find beech nuts, although I was fully aware that mommy could run faster than I could ever dream of running. I told them of the time I'd seen a fisher chase a coyote when it could have chosen to chase me instead.

And then, the next afternoon, as the young folks and I enjoyed lunch, we experienced an animal encounter that left me and my brave reputation undone. The beast appeared out of nowhere, and all my self-control and composure went out the picture window behind me as I clawed at the glass and tried desperately to get away from the creature. (The laws of physics and facts such as "you cannot claw through glass" have no bearing on someone who has lost her mind.)

I climbed onto a chair and squealed in a high-pitched voice, "Kill it! Kill it! Please, God in heaven, please, someone kill it!"

Through the dense cloud of panic, I noticed the faces of the young people as they watched me in shock. All eyes were on me, sandwiches were held motionless en route to open mouths, and concern for my sanity was apparent on frozen faces. Some gave me a pathetic look and shook their heads in bitter disappointment.

The animal escaped, but it was too late. I was thoroughly disgraced—all my brave, bold stories reduced to highly improbable tales of fantasy—by the tiniest of creatures: the mouse.

# Roots

WE DIDN'T KNOW WE WEREN'T COOL. WE SAID THE PLEDGE OF Allegiance to the flag every morning. We ate dog biscuits on a dare. The summers of our childhood weren't about being cool. Feeding chipmunks out of our palms, eating blueberries that we picked from our own wild plants, and finding pink lady's slippers were the things that were important to us.

My childhood summers were spent at "camp" on Moosehead Lake. No matter where my father's military duty took us, he sent Mama, us six kids, and the dog to Greenville, my parents' hometown, for the summer. "So we'd have roots," he said.

I remember arriving for the first time each summer. It was a steep trek from where we parked at the top of the hill to the camp, and as we made our way down the path, Papa's voice caught up to us: "Pick up your feet!" He yelled this to warn us of the entanglement hazard in the large roots that crisscrossed the well-worn trail. I tried to watch my step as I craned my neck around the box of provisions in my arms, but I would inevitably trip on one of the roots—body and box would fly, and the supplies would be scattered.

We spent our summer running around the woods barefoot, eventually learning how to do so without stumbling on the roots. By July my soles had toughened up so I could soar through the forest not even wincing if I stepped on a pinecone, a twig, or a pebble. I would stop only long enough to brush the object away from where it had imbedded itself in my skin.

The days were full of the business of being a child. We played among the tree roots, imagining them our homes. I lived under the pine tree, and my sister lived under the birch. Our play was more creative than Mattel or Fisher-Price ever imagined; we raked and pruned, and the roots became our under-the-tree houses. We had freedom to roam, and Mama seldom checked on us. We had our boundaries and we respected them—the marshy area beside the beach, the fence along the neighbor's property. We were free to wander our wilderness, and we did so with zeal.

The lake was the only thing that could seduce us away from the woods. We were allowed to swim when the thermometer on the front porch reached seventy degrees, and that was the first thing we checked each morning. We burst through the screen door like racehorses out of the gate, and it slammed behind us. The last child out was always chastised; "Close the door ten times quietly!" Mama would yell. The ultimate frustration was, in the rush to join your siblings gathered around the porch post where the thermometer hung, you accidentally slammed the door on the tenth time and Mama thought you did it to be sassy. "Ten more times!" she'd shout from the kitchen. (Mama was always in the kitchen.)

When the temperature and Mama allowed, we would leave the roots of the woods for the freedom of the water. I remember watching my sister hurrying to the lake, doing a bizarre dance as she stepped gingerly on woodland debris, her elbows fanned out like the wings of some strange bird as she attempted to lift her body over the rough ground.

Five of us children, seventeen grandchildren, and seven great-grandchildren live within a day's drive to camp. While we played among the roots of those trees, our feet grew deep roots of their own into the soil of Maine—roots deeper than those of Maine's tallest trees. These roots hold us here like they hold those trees in place. They are like the arms of a loving father that nobody wants to leave. They keep us on this land we love and encircle even the generations that followed. My daughters are Maine women, and my grandsons are Maine boys. My oldest grandson and I recently went to camp for a visit. As I watched him play around those same places where I spent my childhood summers, I could see the roots doing their job, encircling his feet and slowly growing upward to capture his heart.

# Location, Location, Location

My friend Lauren and I went shopping—not at the mall, not even in the city. We went shopping in the willy-wacks. I love (and admit am envious) how some folks have been able to build a life deep in the Maine woods.

As with most of my adventures, this one started out with a plan. Our intention on this day was to visit a friend's garden shop, but curiosity coupled with a penchant for wandering took us down a completely different path. En route to the shop we noticed a sign on the side of the road that read "Bog Pond Pottery."

"That name has a nice ring to it," I said.

"I've always wanted to go there," Lauren said.

"Let's do it." I veered off the paved road onto a dirt road that led us miles into the woods and up a gravel drive to the isolated pottery shop. We found the potter's wood-fired creations stunning, his life unconventional, and his location intriguing, especially for one who wishes to sell his wares. I would later learn (not through him, but through others) that he is internationally known. I suppose if you are as famous as he is, you can sell from anywhere—even from a charming farm on the edge of a wilderness pond deep in the Maine woods. We enjoyed an interesting conversation and were just as fascinated by his life as his art.

Our next stop was to see a close friend of Lauren's. Visiting her meant parking the car and hiking a long, fern-lined forest path, then crossing a swaying suspension bridge decorated with wind chimes and colored streamers, to the backwoods home of this woman who is the most fairylike being I have ever met. That's all I can say without exposing this woodland nymph to the world and possibly destroying hers by that act. Again, I was spellbound by this Mainer's choice of location.

Later, another sign caught our eye: "The Little Boutique in the Woods." Following the signs, we turned off the main road onto a dirt road, took a left onto another dirt road, then a right onto another long, dusty road—all the while passing fields, flowers, and views of the mountain ranges, ponds, rivers, and wildlife. We finally reached the driveway of a private home with a boutique in the barn. Lauren and I looked at each other and said, simultaneously captivated, "There's a boutique in that barn!"

Because the day was over (but not our enjoyment), we headed home, passing by yet another gravel road that meandered up a mountain.

"I have a friend who lives up there," Lauren said.

"Of course you do," I thought.

"He's out of state this week, but we should leave him something to let him know we were here. He has a sculpture of a hand on his porch. We could put something in it."

"Let's leave him this moose tooth," I said and pointed to the offering lying on my dashboard.

"You have a moose tooth in your car?" Lauren asked in amazement.

"You have friends in strange places," I countered.

We drove up the side of the hill to his cabin. The breathtaking view of the Bigelow Mountain Range caused my arms and mouth to open wide. What is it about mountains that can make a person stare with mouth agape and in some cases—like this one—give up plumbing and electricity for a view that stops you in your tracks to anywhere else?

These folks have built their homes and businesses in the middle of nowhere—unless you have the insight to realize that the Maine wilderness is exactly where they should be. They give an entire new meaning to the real estate mantra "location, location, location."

# Why Do I Do This?

I CAN'T EXPLAIN IT; IT'S A MYSTERY, BUT I FEEL COMPELLED TO MOUNTAIN bike. I'm not sure why. As I struggle to bike in this mountainous terrain my thighs burn; my calves and glutes scream for mercy. My heart pounds so hard it makes my teeth ache. I sweat and pant and wish for wings. Even my odometer refuses to work on this rough, uphill journey.

Why do I do this?

The squirrels chuckle at me, and the delicate wildflowers on the side of the road mock me with their effortless, unearned beauty.

"Well, you may be 'pearly everlasting,' but I'm not!" I say to that flower as I pass. "I have to work to stay everlasting for as long as I last!"

To the slope of identical purple lupines I say, "You may have mastered cloning, but once I'm gone—I'm gone!"

A dragonfly in acrobatic flight whizzes past my head and seems to say, "Do it like this! Do it like this! Whee…" then darts off and vanishes into the woods as if he suddenly remembered he left something on at home.

I study a tiny green bug that has hitched a ride on my shirt and is now powerless to detach himself as I speed downhill. I wonder what he would be thinking if he was capable of that action. The way he clutches my sleeve, I find it hard to believe he isn't terrified. I marvel at his fluorescent color and how perfect his tiny form is. I lose my concentration and my precarious hold on the edge of the road and travel onto the soft shoulder. My bike does a wheel-wobble, and an airborne trip into the pucker brush seems imminent, but somehow I manage to stay upright—this time.

Why do I do this?

Farther down the road, I see a spot of brown in a clearing and I stop. It's a huge buck in his prime. I watch him in awe and fascination until my scent reaches him, and with a loud snort the animal dismisses me, turns, and bounds away.

Later, I stop for a drink of water at a bridge that crosses the south branch of the Dead River, and a red-tailed hawk glides overhead looking for his breakfast in the meadow that lines the stream below. He gracefully drifts on the wind in a silent ballet. He gifts me with a feather and I accept it, admiring the intricate colors. I watch him appreciatively until he glides around the bend and out of sight.

I leave the main road for a trail through the woods. My bike bumps over roots, and when my tire hits a hole my teeth slam together. "Why do I do this?" I ask myself. I am reminded by a jolt and a thud as I hit a log that no matter how breathtakingly beautiful the sky is, I should keep my eyes on the path.

A brown rabbit scurries up the bank in front of me. His winter white coloring is left only on his legs, and it looks as if he is wearing socks. When he runs, he looks like a child running wild, an escapee from mom and shoes, and it makes me laugh.

Why do I mountain bike out here in the wilderness even though I'm left with barely enough energy to blink? I'm not sure I can explain it.

# Minor Details

My favorite writer is history. My favorite storyteller is the details. My favorite place is Maine, so this story has all my favorite things.

Maine claims to be the birthplace of the American Navy.

The story goes, in a sign of solidarity with patriots in Lexington and Concord who had recently battled the British, the defiant, fiercely independent citizens of Machias erected a "Liberty Pole." They placed the pole in the middle of town and under the noses of British sea captains who were delivering supplies to the village. The captains were highly indignant at the sight of the pole and refused to unload the goods until it was removed. The people, themselves highly offended at British oppression, refused. A standoff in stubbornness ensued between the two. Patience rarely flows through the veins of rebels, and the townsfolk soon became fed up with waiting. They met and decided to wait for one more thing: for the British officers to go to church that next Sunday. The patriots surrounded the church, captured the officers, seized their ships, then used them to battle and capture two armed schooners that had been sent to escort the supply ships. This was the first naval battle of the soon-to-be American Revolution, and those conquered ships would protect Maine from British occupancy throughout the war.

Therein lies the claim that Maine built the first American Navy, but for me, the following minor details make the story. The year was 1775 so it wasn't Maine yet; it was Massachusetts. And being 1775, it wasn't even America yet. This land was still British America, under British rule. Minor details because those stalwart patriots who dared to cross an ocean for a new life also dared to cross a European empire for that life. I believe it was already set in their hearts and minds that this new land was their land, so those Mainers fought for it and won, and in doing so also won the claim of being the birthplace of the American Navy—because those details that said it was any other land or that they were under anyone else's rule were minor.

## Maine: The Way Life Should Be...Difficult

It's winter here in Maine, and another nor'easter just hit. The home folk are stocking up on food, candles, and firewood, and the smart ones are gathering quilts and good books. We Mainers will weather this storm just fine; this isn't our first go-round.

Since you can't get to Maine by accident (unless you're a lost Canadian), everyone here is here because here is where they want to be (or because they're stuck in the mud, or because summer and fall were so beautiful they forgot to leave and then got stuck in the snow). Most want to be here even if they have to shovel feet of snow out of the way in order to stay put. (My eighty-two-year-old mother shovels her own steps and path to her car.)

Mainers want to be in Maine even though it gets so cold it hurts to breathe deeply, so cold that your toes, fingers, eyeballs, and plumbing freeze. A true Mainiac ignores what the rest of the world thinks and simply chooses the simple life here, which is simple in its assured difficulties. If you choose Maine, you've got to work and work hard; there is no other way. There was a saying in Aroostook County that another birthday only meant your shovel got bigger; those farmers meant the manure shovel, but it's also true of a snow shovel.

There's a sort of pride to surviving here—if you do indeed survive. Some don't. My father told me about an old hermit who lived on Moose Island on Moosehead Lake. It was the hermit's habit to walk across the ice to town for supplies, and on one such trip, as he was returning with large, heavy packages, he fell through the ice up to his armpits. The packages, held in arms spread wide like wings, kept him from going all the way through, but also prevented him from freeing himself. He froze right there in the ice. As an adult, I heard another version. It says his snowshoes—or rather his inability to release the bindings—were his undoing.

I once fell through the ice with snowshoes on. One shoe came off, twisted around my ankle, and attached to something gnarly below the surface. I was tethered in place. It took me a good long time to disentangle myself, and I'm alive today simply because that icy water was only up to my knees. Going for a walk in Maine can be dangerous, but we go anyway. We're ornery like that.

We also have a strange idea of what fun is. I know some Mainers who "just for fun" go out in the wildest of storms for the enjoyment of pulling unfortunate drivers out of ditches or ridding neighbors' driveways of downed trees.

My father loved to go "plowing." He would fill his 1979 Ford F-150 truck with sand, gas, and grandkids and make a day of it. Little did he know he was also making wonderful memories for his grandchildren—memories that have lasted long after he left this world.

Being a successful, year-round Mainer is not easy; it's all in the attitude. And that's the way life should be.

PART TWO

## *Family Is Not Only Why You Are, It's Why You Are the Way You Are*

# A Family Tradition

We have a birthday tradition in our home. It's called "Your once-in-a-lifetime special birthday." It's called that because that's precisely what it is, and it only happens once: the day you turn the age of your birth date. My middle daughter Emily was born on August 11, so she celebrated her once-in-a-lifetime birthday the year she turned eleven. My youngest daughter Holland celebrated hers the year she turned ten, since she was born on April 10. My oldest daughter Kelly was born on March 31. Her once-in-a-lifetime birthday would have to come later, but that's okay because good things come to those who wait, and her celebration promised to be the most memorable of all because adult parties are much more fun.

It took quite a bit of planning, this surprise of surprises, especially because Kelly is and always has been modest and shy and never wants any attention drawn to her. If she had found out about this party in progress, she would no doubt have put an end to it.

It's nearly impossible to keep a secret in this day of social media, but still, it was the best way to contact her long list of friends and our huge family. I invited them all to her favorite sushi restaurant for an extravagant celebration. I explained that Kelly would be turning thirty-one years old on the thirty-first, and how she had waited all these long years for a family tradition. In other words, it would be a big deal—dress up.

On the evening of March 31, I drove her to the restaurant. The parking lot was full of the familiar vehicles of family and friends. I could tell by the look on Kelly's face that she knew.

"Happy special, once-in-a-lifetime birthday!" I smiled at her. "We didn't forget!" I added.

Kelly turned to me with a serious, disapproving look upon her face, but that didn't cause me to think twice. I knew she was about to tsk-tsk me for carrying through with this childhood family tradition— this serious offspring of mine would think it best to put away childish things since she was no longer a child.

"Mother..." She spoke with a tone of displeasure, but I expected that from her. She wouldn't want all this attention.

"Yes, dear?" I was all smiles, ready to defend my actions.

"I'm thirty-two," she said.

I looked at her cockeyed. When the realization of what she was saying hit me, it unhinged my jaw, which dropped. She nodded her head.

"You missed it," she added.

The surprise was on me and all over my face.

I looked toward the restaurant where dozens of dressed-up, excited, and expectant people were waiting to share in Kelly's once-in-a-lifetime, special birthday celebration—a birthday that Kelly had watched come and go, unobserved, a year ago in modest silence. I spoke the only word that came to mind.

"Oops."

# *A Short Story*

SOMEONE SAID, "NECESSITY IS THE MOTHER OF INVENTION." BUT IN OUR family, mothers necessitate the invention of things—unusual things— like the world's shortest stories.

I'll explain shortly.

My oldest daughter thinks her son, Aiden, should get enough sleep, which is why, whenever I visited them when Aiden was a small child, she would sass us for talking too late into the night. Aiden and I were guilty of chatting and storytelling until well past my daughter's bedtime, and she would call from her room, "You two stop talking and go to sleep!"

We tried to obey, but all we truly did was perfect our whispers. Ultimately I felt we had to mind Kelly because even though she is my daughter, she is his mom. This put me in a tight spot between the two of them, a grandson who loves my bedtime stories and a daughter who has the power to silence me with a bedtime banning.

"Tell me a story, Grandmother," Aiden would plea.

"I can't; we'll get in trouble," I'd whisper.

"Just tell me a short one!" he would insist.

To make a long story short, Kelly's shushing led to the invention of the world's shortest stories:

"Once upon a time there was a boy who was so tall nobody knew what he looked like."

"Once upon a time there was a boy who could hit a baseball so hard he only hit them once."

"Once upon a time there was a boy whose room was so messy, nobody could find him."

"Once upon a time there was a boy whose kitchen floor was so sticky it took him a week to get a glass of water."

The details of these tales would play themselves out in Aiden's imagination, and he would fall asleep while the story silently told itself.

Recently we had a family gathering at my daughter's house, and long rides home after dark in winter being what they are, my mom decided to stay overnight. She bunked in with my daughter, and from our bunks in Aiden's room we listened as that grandmother and grandchild's bedtime chatting entered hour number two.

"Grandmother, those two are going to talk all night," Aiden sighed.

"I know," I sighed back. "And there's not a thing we can do about it. They are our moms."

# Mommie Dearest

MOMS ARE BUSY. MOST OF THAT BUSYNESS IS CENTERED ON THE SAFETY of their children. Given the amount of trouble and danger a toddler can get into, if mothers didn't have an insane (almost psychotic) instinct to protect their offspring, not one would grow to adulthood, and the world population would cease. Because of this, mommies—especially modern mommies who work outside the home—have much on their minds. Therefore there are times when Mommie Dearest is the reason a child gets into a precarious situation.

Such was the case with my daughter and her toddler son.

Emily was preparing to leave for work. She tucked Jaxon into his car seat, carefully strapped him in, and to keep him even safer, locked the car doors...with the keys in the ignition. When she realized what she had done, her heart froze in terror.

She frantically called her husband, and with panic nearly seizing her voice, cried, "Oh, my God, Adam, oh my God! I've locked the baby in the van!"

"I'll call you right back," was his response.

Emily was too frantic to wait idly for his return call. She had to do something. (Perhaps if she just kept doing things, the situation would get better.) She called a friend she thought might help. That person didn't answer the phone. She called another and asked if she had access to AAA or some other roadside assistance. She didn't. She called a third friend—again, sympathy, but no help.

Her phone rang; it was hubby. "I called our auto insurance—help is on the way," he said.

"WELL, DID YOU TELL THEM A BABY IS INVOLVED?" Her voice betrayed how close to the edge she was.

"Yes, I told them." He kept his voice calm. (They are, after all, opposites.) "What is Jaxon doing?"

Emily peered into the van window. Jaxon was strapped in his car seat watching his VeggieTales movie, contentedly waiting for his mom to climb in, start the car, and begin the day. (Just like every day.)

Emily answered her hubby, "He's not doing anything. He's watching his movie."

There was silence on the other end of the phone line as Adam tried to piece together the puzzle of crazed mommy-bear brain versus reality.

Emily realized their baby was fine. That's when she understood that it wasn't imminent danger, but the fact that she was no longer in control that caused her terror. As suddenly as the panic had grabbed her, calm settled on Emily. Help arrived; the crisis came to an end—quietly, orderly, and with a lesson to boot.

Emily recounted this story in a letter to me as a way of thanking me for "everything she put me through" as her mom. "I realize there must have been times I frightened or worried you," she said. "And I just want you to know; now that I am a mother, I understand what you went through, and I thank you for taking care of me."

Best Mother's Day gift ever.

# Timeless

THERE IS A SMALL ABANDONED GARAGE ON THE SIDE OF THE ROAD IN Shirley Mills, Maine. I don't think anyone ever notices it sitting there, losing its battle to stay upright, but I notice it—I always have. As a child traveling to our summer home on Moosehead Lake, I watched for that crooked, weather-beaten building with the diamond-shaped window in the center of the door, because seeing it meant I was almost there—almost to my grandmother's camp, to happiness and summer vacation freedom. More than that, the little building meant that a view of the lake was also close. Perhaps, if just this one time my mind didn't get lost in daydreams of the fun days of summer that lay ahead, if just this once I paid attention, maybe I would be the first of the six kids in my family to see the lake as we crested Indian Hill. Being first meant winning our traditional sighting contest and the right to yell, "I see it!" (In later years that would be shortened to "Me!" a one-syllable acceptable way of declaring you were the first to see the lake.)

The prize for winning was the sweetest of all things to a child's taste buds: the right to gloat over your siblings. With a singsong voice you could proclaim, "I saw it first. I saw it first," ignoring the protests of your siblings: "Your head was in my way" or "That's not the lake, that's the roof of the Indian Store."

Of course, someone always accused the winner of cheating. (How anyone could cheat at this contest I could never figure out.)

Mama and Papa had the last word. By authority of the front seat, they decided if it was indeed a false sighting, or if some other violation had occurred, like the time my sister crammed a travel pillow into my face at the crucial moment.

We played that game for many years, well into young adulthood.

* * *

My maternal great-grandmother, Delia Mandanda Snowdale, grew up in the town of Weston in southern Aroostook County. She wrote this childhood memory in her journal dated 1890: "When we lived out on what they called the Calais Road, about five miles from where Grandmother lived, there was quite a piece of woods. I can remember several times walking out there with Mother and Father. When we came out of the woods we were way up on a hill, a quarter mile from Grandfather's. When you got to a certain place you could look down over a field and you could see the house. I remember when we would get out of the woods my oldest brother Thaddeus and I would start running to see who would get a sight of the house first."

My great-grandmother raced out of the woods onto the top of a hill to view the prize—her grandparents' house. We crested a different hill to win sight of a different prize, Moosehead Lake.

I can hear Delia's singsong voice now. "I see it, Thaddeus! I see Grandmother's!" I can hear her voice as clearly as I remember my own. "I see it; I see the lake!"

Some childhood games are timeless.

# Vitals

A FEW YEARS AGO I WAS VISITING MY GREAT-AUNT WHO WAS TURNING ninety-five years old. I smiled and told her, "Aunt Sarah, I do believe you will live to be one hundred." She granny-slapped me. (It stung like the dickens.)

"Don't you dare wish that on me!" she said. "I do NOT want to be known as 'Sarah who lived to be one hundred'!"

As it turns out, she won't be remembered that way, she'll be remembered as "Sarah who lived to be one hundred and four." She turned that age about a week ago. Actually, she's lived one hundred and five years, but given Sarah's mood on the subject, I think it best not to bring that up.

I visited her recently at the nursing home in Greenville. Her body is slow, but her mind is quick. Our conversation eventually turned to what matters most to most elderly: their health.

"You know we have vitals, right?" she asked.

"Yes, Aunt Sarah, I know we have vitals," I said. (I guessed Aunt Sarah had forgotten I was a nurse.)

"Well, I get a bath every Tuesday, and they take my vitals. And..." I could hear a bit of elderly annoyance creeping into her shaky voice, "...there isn't anything wrong with them! My blood pressure, my pulse, my cholesterol—nothing is wrong! I don't have anything that will kill me!" She was fully perturbed now and stomped her cane to emphasize it.

"That's a good thing, isn't it?" I asked.

She shook her head. "I really don't understand what God is waiting for!" (Did I mention she's also a bit spicy?)

"Aunt Sarah, it's just not time for you to leave us," I said.

"Well," she was quick to reply, "I get bored in the afternoons!"

I can understand that. I hate being bored in the afternoon. If you get bored in the morning, you can start a big project. If you get bored in the evening, you can call it a day and climb into a comfy chair with a good book and a warm quilt. But what is one to do with boredom in the afternoon except suffer through it?

Sarah explained that her eyesight was failing. She could no longer read, which left her hands and her afternoons empty, nothing to behold while on divine hold, empty fingers while she lingered, that sort of thing. She had too much empty space in her day. Unacceptable! Too much empty space is not a good thing—it leaves way too much room for bad things to slither in, things like discontent, which leads to discouragement and despair.

Little tiny nursing home room space or wide open wilderness space, all space should be full of something interesting, something stimulating, something stirring, or something beautiful—these things are vital to a healthy life.

"How about if we get you set up with books on tape while you wait?" I suggested. She had no idea there was such a thing, and the thought of being read to filled her with excitement once again. I spoke to the activities director, who was more than willing to set her up with an audio library. Now Sarah is wearing a smile again because she's wearing headphones.

I hope the fascinating fantasies, the lovely thoughts of poets, and the comforting words of writers keep her vitals strong for another year...or even longer.

# *Caught*

I RECENTLY FOUND MYSELF DRIVING AROUND MY OLD STOMPING GROUNDS and discovered that while doing so, memories come back around, too.

I drove by a little neighborhood market that I used to walk past on my way to and from school. It became a habit for my friends and me to stop into the store and spend whatever small change we happened to have in our pockets. We were not yet of the employable age, so that was often just a few coins. My friends and I would huddle together outside the market's doors, and that is where we were the day my secret was found out.

My siblings and I were brought up to be cognizant of the effects that inhaled, ingested, and indecent habits had on our minds and bodies, and we were habitually educated by my parents not to partake in the world's harmful ways.

So, before I tell you about the day I was caught, I ask you please, do not judge me. I hope you remember what it was like to be a young person in the middle of a group of your peers—a difficult place to take a stand, and while standing there, it's easier to go with the flow to keep the peace. That's the way it is, or was, in my case, anyway.

So there I was with my friends, partaking of one of those harmful indulgences when a car drove in and illuminated us. It was my father. There I was, his little dear caught in the headlights. And caught I was because I was holding contraband. With no way to trash it unnoticed, I quickly hid it behind my back. Papa motioned for me to get into the car. I did. I held my box of "shouldn't-haves" in the hand that was lowered between the seat and the door. He noticed I was trying to hide something, but he didn't speak.

You know how it is when you're trying to hide something? The thing you're hiding takes on a life of its own and works all the harder to become known. That's what happened next. My box of shame dropped from my hand and made a slight thump as it hit the floor. Papa's eyebrow—the one closest to me—went up.

I turned my face toward the window. If I looked away, perhaps the uncomfortable situation would go away, too. (I've learned that never works.)

Papa broke his silence. "I drove by here the other day and saw a young girl in a group just like this one." He pointed at my friends with his chin. "That girl was smoking a cigarette and drinking a beer." His voice was flat; his expression, sober. "She looked just like you." He hesitated, then continued, "Was it you?"

I didn't hesitate. "No, Papa, it wasn't me." He wasn't convinced, and although I knew I was done for, I wasn't going to give up my stash and freedom voluntarily. He'd have to demand and confiscate. He did.

"Let's have them." He held out his hand.

I steadied myself for the disapproval, along with a lecture and the scowl…maybe I'd be grounded…

There was nothing left for me to do but to hold up and hand over my sin: a box of Milk Duds candy.

Papa was stunned into silence. He couldn't enjoy relief because of his confusion. He looked at the box. He looked at me. One worry was replaced by another. I could read his thoughts. "Why are you hiding candy? What is wrong with this kid of mine that she hides candy like it's a box of nuclear missiles…or cigarettes?"

He shook his head and drove us home.

Well, Mama always said not to eat junk food.

# When Worlds Collide

ONE BOY IS JUST LEARNING TO WALK; HE TEETERS AND TOTTERS AND occasionally crashes into walls, cabinets, furniture, or the floor. The other boy is older and is also learning to travel, but this one travels by truck. He too crashed—into a ditch after the vehicle rolled over twice! The boys are bruised and battered, but they will heal, and probably faster than the nerves of their poor parents.

These wrecks, these boys, are my grandsons. Jaxon is one year old, and Aiden is sixteen. Their ages and their modes of transportation are the only differences between them, because the result was the same—they crashed!

When we try something new and tricky we may get banged up, but we learn. Hopefully (prayerfully) we learn well enough and early enough so we can live long enough to have kids and then watch them survive life's collisions.

Aiden showed me a result of his car accident: a two-inch scar above his left eye.

"It looks like you had a lobotomy," I said.

"Good one, Grandmother," he grumbled.

"Did you learn anything from this experience?" I asked.

"Stop when you are supposed to," he mocked.

"Good one, Aiden," I said.

It's a good thing these boys are hard-headed since they seem to have a tendency to fall off things—like roads and their feet.

I'm not saying my three daughters were—are—crash-proof, far from it. As a matter of fact, Aiden's mother totaled her car after having it a mere three weeks, so he beat her total time by almost seven days. My middle daughter had her driver's license for twenty minutes when she sideswiped a utility pole and caused eight thousand dollars in damages to my car. My car was never the same, but neither was she; she became a better, more attentive driver. After their accidents, both girls became cautious behind the wheel. I called these episodes their crash courses in learning.

Like Jaxon, my youngest daughter also falls off her feet. She is a snowboarder and has crashed more times than she can count. I, however, remember exactly how many falls landed her in the emergency room: two. But with every snowboarding trick that ended badly, she came back stronger and more knowledgeable than before.

There is a new grandbaby due in the spring. No doubt he will crash into this world headfirst and collide with all sorts of things as he goes through life; that's a given. Each landing may not be softer than the one before, for it's a truism that the bigger they are, the harder they fall. The hope is the experience will land them in a better, more capable place.

## *Who Rules the House?*

THERE ARE A LOT OF RULES INVOLVED WHEN YOU ARE RAISING THREE daughters to become responsible adults with proper etiquette. My youngest daughter, Holland, took it upon herself to instruct her sisters Kelly and Emily, who are nine and seven years older than she.

I found this list of rules in a box in the attic, written by a then seven-year-old Holland to her teenage sisters.

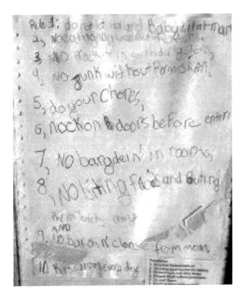

Rule 1: Do not lot Holland babysit at Mammy's.

2, No eating anywhere but the kichen

3, no trackin' in with dirty shoes,

4, no junk without permishan,

5, do your chores,

6, nock on doors before enterin'

7, no bardgein' in rooms,

8, no biting fruits and putting them back, (emily)

9. no baroin' close from mom.

10. Kiss m♥m everyday.

NOTE: *mispellings reflect the original document*

THE TRANSLATION FOR THOSE WHO NEED IT:

Do not let Holland babysit at Mammy's. (Mammy is my mother, and all the grandchildren spent a lot of time at her place, where the older grandchildren often babysat the younger. I'm not sure what this rule meant; I can only guess that either Kelly or Emily shirked her duties and left Holland in charge, with disastrous results.)

No eating anywhere but the kitchen. (No one ever paid attention to this rule.)

No tracking in with dirty shoes.

No junk [food] without permission.

Do your chores.

Knock on doors before entering.

No barging in the rooms. (My personal favorite.)

No biting fruits and putting them back (Emily). (I wondered which kid was doing that.)

No borrowing clothes from Mom. (Nobody ever paid attention to this rule either—they still don't.)

Kiss Mom every day. (Notice the heart in place of the *o*? Some types of kisses aren't so sweet. It's a good thing the kid was adorable.)

These rules seem appropriate, no matter how inappropriate it was for a little Miss Bossy Pants with a spelling problem to write them to her sisters. But appropriate or not, I hung them over the guestbook table in my bed and breakfast for all my guests to read…and heed.

# Girl Hunting

THANKSGIVING WAS NEVER A BIG DEAL AT OUR HOME. OUR FAMILIES spent that holiday weekend hunting for food and big deals. The men went up in the woods, and the gals went to the mall.

My father would take all his grandsons up to camp for the long weekend to go bird and deer hunting. My daughter Kelly, the oldest of ten granddaughters, decided things should be different. At around the age of ten, Kelly noticed all her male counterparts got to go with their grandfather, Pappy, and decided that wasn't fair. Why should all her male cousins get to go? After all, the guys were going to her daddy's logging camp at Elm Pond. She of all people should be there! "Pappy should invite me!" she asserted. I promised to mention it to my father.

"Kelly wants to go hunting with you and the boys this year," I told him.

"Kelly wants to go hunting?" His expression was easy to decipher. My statement didn't match up with this little dress-wearing, frilly-filly child who played with Barbie and baby dolls all day. Pappy was skeptical that Kelly wanted to spend a long weekend at hunting camp with a mess of stinky guys. He was thoughtful for a moment and then explained, "I never asked her because I didn't think she'd be interested in going."

But this was the father and grandfather who believed his girls should be allowed to wear whatever shoes they chose: hiking or hunting boots, high heels...or both. So, as the end of November neared, he invited Kelly to join the guys on the upcoming hunting trip. Kelly gave him one of those heart-melting hugs that can only come from a child and answered, "Oh, no thanks, Pappy. I don't like hunting, but thank you for asking."

As Papa and I watched her skip away it dawned on us: she only wanted to be asked; she wanted to be included.

Every year after that, Pappy invited his granddaughters to hunt with him. Some politely declined, but some became hunters.

# Granny Rules

My daughter is going to be a mom. (The truth is because she's pregnant, she's already a mother.) She is a mom waiting to see her son's face, and I noticed the other day she was holding her belly—her first embrace of motherhood.

This child will be grandchild number one for her mother-in-law, who, because I have a grandchild, teasingly asked me to explain the "grandmother" rules. I told her, "Grandmother rules are the opposite of the traditional parenting rules."

## We Are Yes Ma'ams

My phone rang; it was my daughter telling me that my grandson Aiden wanted to come for a visit.

"Well, of course! I would love that," I said. "Bring him."

"No, Mom, you don't understand—he can't. You have to tell him no."

I immediately prickled. "Now just one minute! I don't ever have to tell that child 'no'—I'm the grandmother!"

How many times in his life does a child hear the word *no*? According to one UCLA survey, the average toddler hears it up to four hundred times a day! Think about it; when we said "no" to a child, wasn't it our habit to say "No, no, no"?

This means that as a mother of three, collectively I've said "no" over a thousand times a day for many years. I think it's high time both the child and I hear nothing but "yes."

## *We Are Quilts*

On another occasion, Aiden called me.

"Well, Grandmother," he sighed, "I'm grounded."

"What happened?" I asked. (It is important to note that I didn't ask "What did you do?" Every grandmother understands that her grandchild is absolutely innocent, merely a victim of circumstances.)

"I set off a stink bomb in study hall and made all the girls cry."

"Who gave you a stink bomb?" (Notice again, it's presumed that the circumstances are not of his making.)

"A friend," he said. "His grandmother gave them to him!"

"Well," I educated him, "she's completely within her rights to buy whatever she chooses for her grandson. What he does with her gift is on his own head."

"But the worst part is I'm going to miss opening day of hunting season."

I responded in the most grandmotherly appropriate way. "Would you like me to make you a caramel apple pie, Sweetie?" I asked.

He sighed, "Yes, I think that will make me feel better."

"And how about if I make you some of your favorite pumpkin bread?" I offered.

"Yes, Grandmother, that would help, too."

His parents and the school authorities are handling the discipline, leaving me free to be the comforter. I love that. I had to discipline my children for their good; it feels like this is a heavenly reward for carrying out that responsibility.

## *We Are 911*

"Grandmother, come and get me!" It was a very young, very angry Aiden on the line.

"I'm putting on my boots; what's the matter?" (It is noteworthy that I am willing to immediately drop everything and run to the rescue.)

I learned that Aiden was unhappy with a parental decision and was attempting a mutiny of Tom Sawyer proportions. I spoke to him soothingly and after finding out what was upsetting him, applied the grandmother "opposite rules" again and agreed with everything he said.

"Yes, rules are the pits. And yes, I hate rules, too! I had to write thank-you notes," I told him. "To everyone, for everything!"

"Bummer," he said.

"Well, it was a rule. And, you know, Aiden—it really was the right thing to do."

It calmed him down to know someone was on his side (even if he was wrong). And in doing so, it helped him feel a little more in control, and feeling in control will soothe the most savage beast.

Grandparents Day is the second Sunday in September. Enjoy your grandchildren with freedom.

# Thanks, Bro

ALTHOUGH WE GREW UP IN THE SAME HOUSEHOLD, MY OLDER BROTHER and I were worlds apart. We were so different. He was smart—and by smart I mean MENSA brilliant—but I was average. We got along fine; that wasn't the issue. As a matter of fact, we loved each other and stood up for each other. It was a case of him not having much in common with my common and unremarkable intellect. This was not a bad thing, nor was it a good thing; it was simply how it was. Over the course of our childhoods, I learned some significant things from him—stuff that the most common person probably knew but had slipped my notice. Like sideburns and snake holes and downshifting my mother's Volkswagen Fastback.

When it was time for us to learn to drive, Papa insisted we learn on a car with a manual transmission, probably for the man-to-machine symbiosis. I was always relieved to get through the first three gears so I could cruise along easily in fourth.

I remember driving my mother's car on the Wilson Pond Road, north of Greenville. I don't remember why my brother was the passenger, but I do remember the exasperation in his voice when he'd had enough of his body jerking back and forth and demanded, "Downshift!" Once I did, it made sense. Until then it hadn't occurred to me that the gears go down as well as up. I'm sure I thought downshifting was the equivalent to walking downstairs backward. My brother taught me the power that comes with downshifting and how not to look like such a jerk. I can drive anything now and I do—with confidence. Thanks, Bro.

When we were post-pubescent wannabes, we yearned to be just like the icons of the day. Elvis Presley and Burt Reynolds had resurrected the Civil War-era fashion of sideburns. I was telling a story about an adolescent friend who I thought had the coolest sideburns in school, although a razor had yet to touch the baby-smooth skin of his face.

"Hair grown long in front of the ears is not a true sideburn," my brother noted. "Real sideburns are whiskers."

That day, my brother impressed upon me the importance of details. One fact, even a minor one, can change an entire story. Cool, Bro; thank you.

And then there were times he was just being a brother.

One night I stood on my pillow and tiptoes, pulling myself up by the fingertips to raise my eyes just above the windowsill. I stared out into the vast, barren darkness that was our new backyard in Oklahoma.

"Do you see those mounds of dirt?" my brother asked me.

I nodded my four-year-old head.

"And do you see those holes in those mounds?"

I did.

"Those are snake holes, and if you go out there, you're so little, you'll probably fall into one."

I can't ever go outside. Okay, Bro. Thanks for that.

Well, mostly he was helpful.

# Spoiler Alert

SANTA CLAUS CAME TO OUR HOUSE WHEN I WAS SIX YEARS OLD. WELL, he had visited our home in previous years, but the year I was six, I was awake when he arrived.

I was playing on the floor in the living room when a big man with a fat white beard and red clothing came to the door. I recognized him immediately. I also recognized that right in front of me was proof of his existence. The skeptics could forever be silenced, for there he was.

I was excited; I was in awe. My overwhelmed heart pounded in my tiny chest. I was the best little girl in the world. This was going to be the best Christmas of my life!

Santa sat in our living room and passed out gifts to the six of us kids as we sat around his knees.

And then I noticed his gift bag. I thought it strange; it looked very much like my mother's laundry sack that hung from a hook in the cellarway. My focus was redirected.

"If that is Mama's laundry bag," I thought to myself, "then this is a bag of dirty tricks!"

My eyes hardened. My heart narrowed. I needed to know; I could think of nothing else. I wanted this distribution of coloring books and crayons to be over with so I could investigate.

Finally, Santa stood up to leave, and I did the same. But I didn't leave slowly, I ran. So did my siblings. They were suspicious, too! We ran to the door that opened into the cellar. My father, reading our minds, bolted past and blocked it with legs and arms wide, but my smallness was finally advantageous to my will. As my father attempted to block six little monkeys as they tried to climb over, around, or through him, I squiggled past in that space between his outstretched arm and his hip.

And there it was, smack dab in front of me again—the real truth, or rather the lie—revealed by an empty hook in a cold, dark cellarway. Santa had Mama's laundry bag! The only way that was possible was if my parents were involved. The meaning of this slowly seeped into my understanding, into my childhood. Papa tried to salvage the situation. He said Santa was just borrowing it.

No, Papa. Stop trying. The gig is up. It's over. There is no such thing as Santa Claus.

Did it affect me to learn I had been good for no reason all those years? That I had been good for nothing?

Nah. I'm pretty sure I was born cynical.

I have a friend who, upon learning the truth of the lie, decided it would be wise to share her discovery with her classmates during show-and-tell. What a naughty little girl. She didn't get on Santa's list that year. She regrets that to this day—not that she found out the truth, but that she shared it.

Be assured—the truth will be discovered, and it will spread.

Now, here's something that isn't a secret: eventually, every child finds out the truth. So Mom, Dad, be careful. There is a possible and devastating consequence that could ruin your holiday: if your kids find out about Santa, they may start wondering about Elf on the Shelf.

# Family Lines

PERHAPS IT WAS BECAUSE OF PRESIDENTS' DAY. MAYBE IT WAS BECAUSE I'm a history buff (especially American history and personal family history). Whatever the reason, I was recently reading about Abraham Lincoln and my ancestry—not that the two are related.

I enjoy the personal stories I discover. Like finding out that my Scottish great-great-great-great-great-grandfather was friends with the poet Robert Burns. This means nothing now, of course; it's just interesting. I don't even like the poems of Robert Burns. That's my shortcoming, I'm sure. It's undoubtedly because Burns wrote in the Scottish dialect of the 1780s, and I only understand about every fifth word.

Another fascinating discovery was learning that there is gold buried on the family farm. They say that my great-great-grandfather buried his gold on his farm in Kouchibouguac, Canada, but he never told anyone where it was. While he lay dying on his bed, he attempted to tell people something important, but they were unable to make out his words. They believe he was trying to tell them where he buried his treasure. Can you imagine the look on their faces when he breathed his last and they realized the secret stayed just that?

The most fascinating discovery was learning how close I came to not being. During my recent trip to the past, I discovered Abraham Lincoln, one of our country's best loved and greatest men, does not have any direct descendants. Three out of four of Abe's children died in childhood, and his family line ended in 1985 when his childless great-grandson died. That is very similar to my family history. All six children of my great-great-great-grandmother died, most in childhood, from various diseases—the only saving grace being that one lived long enough to sire a child before she died of tuberculosis at the age of thirty. My family very narrowly escaped going the way of Lincoln's. Given the almost incomprehensible span of time—the years, the decades, the centuries, the millenniums—amazingly it was one fragile yet successful nine-month gestation period, a mere nine months of health out of all that time, is the reason I'm alive. Also, taking into consideration the incidence of disease, human frailty, and my party-hearty younger years, it's a wonder I lived to adulthood. But I did. That makes me pause and realize it's a miracle I'm sitting here writing this. Do you understand what a miracle it is that you're sitting there reading it?

# The Good Mom Award

THERE WILL BE TIMES WHEN TRYING TO DO THE BEST FOR OUR CHILDREN won't just be our goal, but our defense when our parenting fails.

My family seems to be plagued with a genetic weakness where the health of our teeth is concerned, so when I read about a trick to make sure the children were brushing their teeth for a full two minutes (the time recommended by most dentists), I was eager to give it a try. The article suggested using a sand timer. "What a brilliant idea!" I thought. I didn't have a sand timer, but one of my kids had a tube timer that dripped gel from the top of a cylinder to the bottom in an oil-based liquid. I dug the timer out of the toy box and set it on the sink in their bathroom.

This was going to be great. This was going to make my parental monitoring responsibilities a little easier. I was sure my children would never think to pull some of the lazy, rebellious stunts I did—like wetting my toothbrush and putting it back in the holder without it ever touching my mouth—but just in case…

That evening, I instructed my little girls to brush their teeth until all the gel in the timer had run down. Then I left them to it and went back to my busy mom work. After a few minutes, I heard a toothpaste-soaked call from the bathroom, but I was determined to win the good mom award at their upcoming dental appointment and called back, "Brush until the timer has run out, please!"

Again, a bit later, "Mom!"

It was the end of a day of battles—there had been an argument with a coworker, frustration with the computer, aggravation with the continual low tire pressure on the right front tire, and a hundred other minor molehill annoyances that had piled up, one on top of the other, to create a mountain climb that had left me exhausted. I was tired and wanted the scrimmages to end.

I yelled to the girls, "NO arguing!"

There was silence—a long silence—and my mommy alarm

sounded at the no-noise level. I checked on them. They were sitting on the edge of the tub obediently (albeit not enthusiastically) brushing their teeth. A lot of time had passed, but not all the gel in the timer had. Upon investigation, I discovered that it was a twenty-minute timer.

Poor little girls and their bleeding gums. So much for the good mom award.

I recently asked my now adult daughter if she remembered this incident. She did not. Although it haunts me, she has no recollection and seems not to have been affected by it. The other daughter recently sent me a Mother's Day card touting a parental job well done because, as the card read, she is neither a stripper nor in prison. I guess she too survived her childhood (although I wonder about her cynicism).

Where were the two-minute fun videos that help with toothbrush timing when I needed them? Why hadn't Dr. Fresh invented the one-minute flashing-light toothbrush when my kids were little?

Above all else, parents are human. We fail, but thankfully, sometimes our kids forget those failures, hopefully because the good outweighs the bad. I find comfort in reminding myself that the unintended cruelty inflicted on them that day wasn't nearly as bad as the time I accidentally murdered their pet mice.

As a parent, I tried. I did my best, and I did what I thought was best for my kids. That's my defense.

# A Sweet Memory

MY PATERNAL GRANDPARENTS OWNED A SMALL NEIGHBORHOOD MARKET in Greenville, Maine. It belonged to both of them, but my grandmother was rarely in the store. She was usually in the house, in the kitchen, near the wood-burning Glenwood cookstove. My father told me that when he was a boy, Grammy would put kittens in the oven to keep them warm and alive. I used to stare at that stove and wonder how she did that without cooking them, but I never asked for fear of what would be thought of my thoughts.

My grandfather was in the store from the moment the doors opened until he locked them at night. If Grampy wasn't too busy, we were allowed to go see him. The back of the store was attached to their home by a covered walk, and the door opened into a room where boxes were piled high over my head—boxes of paper towels, toilet tissue, pet food, and I don't know what else waiting to be placed on the shelves out front.

It seems to me Grampy was always standing behind the meat counter in his white, blood-stained apron, cleaver in hand and in front of a wall of photographs of him and state politicians or important people. The people in the pictures were shaking hands with one another but smiling in a different direction at the camera, and I remember wondering about that, too. Grampy was the only one in those photos I cared about. I loved him, not just because he was my grampy and I was his namesake, but because he once told my mother I was a gem. Although he was a gentle, kind man, he wasn't overly demonstrative with his love, so to me, that spoke volumes. It's important for a little girl to know she's a gem in someone's eyes.

Once in the store, we were allowed one piece of candy and a soda. I don't remember what candy I chose, but I remember the soda I wanted, craved, thirsted after. We weren't allowed sugary drinks at home, so this once-in-a-while treat was like dew from heaven for the parentally parched. Cream soda was my choice every single time. I don't know when I first tasted one, but once I did I was hooked on the sweet vanilla flavor.

I think back with special fondness on the soda machine. The bottle tops were visible through the glass on the door, and all those colorful caps advertised the names: Coke, Moxie, Root Beer, and Orange. I remember the anticipation I felt when I opened that door, grasped a bottle by the neck, and gave it a yank. It resisted a bit as I tugged, but with one confident "Grampy-said-I-could-have-you" authoritative pull, it would give way. It was free.

I don't remember exactly when I stopped going to Grampy's store for a treat. It was sometime between when I was six years old and thirty-six years ago this month, when he passed away. Another thing I don't remember is when I stopped drinking cream soda, but I did. For some reason I'm craving one now, remembering how sweet it was, as sweet as the memory of going to Grampy's store.

# *A Memory*

"STOP PEELING THE BARK OFF THE BIRCH TREES!"

I jumped away from my sin and ran from the man who had rebuked me, venturing deeper into the woods that surrounded our summer home on Moosehead Lake.

"You're going to kill every blasted one!" my maternal grandfather yelled at my disappearing backside as I ran for our lives (mine and the trees).

No matter where my father's military career took us, my family returned to our camp on Moosehead Lake every summer of my childhood, and I returned to peeling the bark off the birches. I can't explain it; I couldn't help myself. The flesh beneath was perfect, smooth, and fresh. Plus, the birches were easy to peel. There was just something special about the feeling of peeling.

I worked on perfecting my ability to peel unnoticed, by standing on the side of the tree away from the cabin and my grandfather's view and admonishment. But I could never get away with anything— I was always found out and corrected.

My grandfather wasn't a mean old man, just an old man, and that is what I called him: Man. And I loved that man. All his gruffness melted away when I put my arms around his neck. I think his grumpiness was a shield to protect his very tender heart—sort of like the hard candy shell that covers the soft chocolate inside an M&M.

Man only hollered at me on a few occasions, like when I was a teenager and stole one of his cigarettes, and again when he caught me kissing a boy. (That boy ran like he'd been caught peeling bark off a birch.)

On a recent visit back to Moosehead, I was swinging in the hammock in front of our family's summer home. My knees were up, and my heels dug into the ropes to hold me in place. On the upswing, I saw the birch trees over the tops of my kneecaps. I swung and stared—knees, trees, knees, trees, knees, trees...and I remembered my grandfather and that small memory from my childhood that gives me a big smile now.

My grandfather has been gone for a long time, but those birch trees are still there, tall, strong, standing. They remind me of him and our time together. Little wonder he wanted them to live.

# Night Sounds Like Childhood

MY BEDROOM WINDOW WAS OPEN WHEN I WENT TO BED LAST NIGHT, AND after listening to the chorus of peepers and crickets for a while, I was reminded of what it was like growing up in a house full of kids: noisy. I heard a dog bark in the distance. Yes, that would be Mama, barking at us to "Keep it down to a dull roar!"

Our playroom was in the basement—a wonderfully spacious area with room and freedom to grow, and grow we did, through our well-fed imaginations. Those were the days of secret agents, and one of our favorite pastimes was to bring the then-popular TV show "The Man from U.N.C.L.E." to life. My brother was the lead secret agent Napoleon Solo, and my tomboy sister was his second in command, Illya Kuryakin. My mind's eye can picture them running to, hiding behind, and shooting from the three-section couch that they had rearranged and upended.

I was the girl they rescued. (I always had to be the girl.) We spent a lot of time in the basement—sometimes too long. Once, when I didn't come up for a while, Mama asked my sister if she had seen me.

"Yes," she answered. "She's down in the basement, rolled up in a rug."

My brother had rolled me up inside a heavy, room-sized braided rug and left me there (to rot, I imagine). To this day I can't stand tight places.

Lying in bed last night, I noticed that the peepers would fall into immediate silence when a car drove past. That was just like us, too. We would drop our toys and voices and run to the window, our noses just above the sill, to see who had driven in. I suppose because there were so many of us, we didn't go visiting much, so it was a big deal to get company.

A cow from my neighbor's farm mooed a long, low, deep vocal sound, and I thought of my father back in those days. I remember him sitting in the living room, one ankle across his knee, smoking his pipe and reading.

"Papa, how old are you?" I once asked him. I ran to my room and cried like a little girl at his answer, certain and terrified that I was to lose him any day to old age because he was so advanced in years. He was thirty-two. That seemed ancient to me, a mere girl of six.

I looked out the window, the stars above twinkled, and I thought, "Childhood is like a twinkle of a star: it shines as bright and is gone as fast. It's nice to remember those sweet and fleeting days, but I have adult things to do in the morning, a lot of mature, responsible, grown-up work to do. I need to be rested. I need my sleep!"

"Enough of this," I told myself.

I got up and closed the window.

But I didn't lock it.

# Crazy Days

MY YOUNGEST DAUGHTER HOLLAND IS GETTING MARRIED THIS SUMMER. Bring on the crazy.

It seems crazy to me that she is old enough to bat an eye at a guy, much less marry one. And it seems crazy that a wedding costs so much! Yikes. I may have to sell my birthright, although anyone willing to buy into this family during this crazy time would have to be... nuts.

There are so many details to attend to. Craziest of all is the amount of running around we are doing to make this day the one she has dreamed of and wished for. Just when I think everything is under control, someone asks a question that I don't know how to answer, like, "Who is performing the ceremony?" I have forgotten that detail and I wonder if the bride has forgotten, also. The frantic texts and phone calls fly. As it turns out, of course she knows who is presiding over her nuptials, then I feel silly for fretting. Fretting is a big part of the crazy.

And then there are her sisters. Her dear, loving sisters who were seven and nine years old when she was born; they were the perfect ages for wanting a real live doll. They have been her second mothers from the moment she entered this world. Actually, I was the second mother; they were the first, proven by what Holland called me when she was a toddler: "Other-mum." I was just her babysitter while Kelly and Emily were at school. Holland's wedding gives them another opportunity to play baby doll, and they relish the chance to once again dress her up and do her hair. Naturally, they will help pick out her dress, but I'll pay for it, of course, which seems crazy, but fair—after all, they raised her. (Maybe they should wear the mother-of-the-bride dresses.)

There are times when the wedding ideas flow so fast during these crazy planning days that I can only keep up by seeing what my girls have pinned to one another's boards on the online bulletin board

Pinterest. They certainly are enjoying this insane process, and that's the fun part for me—watching them. They are taking all summer to prepare for one day, this one day that is the beginning of all my little girl's hopes and dreams.

And what do I hope for her?

My hope for my daughter is not for happiness, because happiness is a temporary feeling. Happiness is like having a sugar high that needs to be continually fed in order to stay maintained. Instead, I wish her a continual state of peaceful existence, and that is found only in contentment. Contentment isn't a hungry beast like happiness. Being content is a whole, multigrain, balanced diet that metabolizes evenly and steadily, a diet that builds muscle so that when those happy times wane, the skeleton—the framework—remains solid and intact.

Of course I want my child, my children, to have mountains of happiness—happy times that rise atop a solid ground built on contentment. That is what I hope for my child and her choice.

That's not crazy, is it?

# I Want to Go Back

If I were given the chance to travel in time, and offered the choice to go to the future or the past, I would normally choose to go forward, to what will be. Yesterday, I would have chosen that direction, but today, I want to go back. I want to return to the days my grandmother said were the best of my life, but I was too busy to notice. I want to go back to the days when my daughters were little girls. Nanny was right; those were the best days of my life, and yes, I was too busy to know it. I'm not going to pine away about how I would take more time with my children, clean the house less, work less, or play more...most of us want that, right? That's a no-brainer.

I want to go back, not to participate, or to change anything, not even to see the things that need changing. I don't wish to relive the past because that chapter of my life is written—and published—in them. Those chapters have no rewrites, no editing; they are finished.

I want to revisit those days to simply sit down beside their childhoods and watch them. I want to sit on the edge of their young lives and watch them grow—like the times we climbed the rocks alongside Route 15 to sit quietly and view the world. I want to witness their childhoods bloom to maturity. I want to watch the angels before they grew wings.

I want to see them dance.

I want to watch them while they sleep; to see their little chests rise and fall with life. This time I won't need to sleep when they do; I'm not tired from chasing them anymore.

I want to go back to enjoy the challenges I couldn't then because they were...challenges. I want to hear their arguments—to hear what logic and the defense they used when they fought. I'm sure it would be as hilarious now as it was serious then. It wouldn't be necessary for me to intervene or to teach peace, for I would be just an observer.

I want to go back to sit and listen to them. I want to hear them sing. I can't reminisce on these things because I don't remember all the details. I was so busy conducting the orchestra, I failed to hear some of the music.

I want to see again every single moment I saw then and every single moment I missed.

My youngest daughter Holland is a newlywed. She is my last little minion, now married like her older sisters. I'm happy for her and her choice, afraid for her, excited for her. Holland's marriage will be wonderful, joyful, and precious, like her childhood. But, alas, her marriage makes me yearn for her little-girlhood.

I want to go back.

## *Butterflies in the Garden*

Your children's lives are like butterflies in the garden.

You spend most of your time and energy making that garden a safe, nurturing place for them. You are so busy watching them flutter from flower to flower—stage to stage—feeding them, clothing them, teaching them, making a home for them, and keeping them alive, that it isn't until they have flown away—left you for a grown-up garden—that you think back and realize, "Wow, that was beautiful."

PART THREE:

*Faith, Hope, and Love*

## Minus Six Degrees

I STOOD AS CLOSE TO THE STOVE IN MY KITCHEN AS I DARED WHILE I squirmed into my clothing. Balancing precariously on one foot, I inserted the other into the leg of my jeans. The trick is to stay close enough to the heat so as not to feel the cold on your bare skin, yet far enough away so as not to feel the burn.

It was at that moment I remembered my mother telling me how she and her brother dressed for school behind the coal stove in their kitchen. Back then warmth was an expensive luxury because of the Great Depression, and I'm sure the heat in their home was scant. I am cold not because the heat in my home is scanty, but because my clothes are. I don't like long johns and layers and bulk. But living in Maine in minus-six-degree weather means I have to layer up. Sometimes I am under so many layers that I can't tie my boots or buckle my seatbelt, and it seems the only body part that can freely move is my eyeballs. On top of that, I despise the way I look in a winter hat!

In an effort to keep every inch of skin protected from the cold winter air, I have nearly perfected the art of getting dressed under my jammies—which is to say, I can get dressed without getting undressed. It's really quite a sight to NOT behold.

I had a college professor once tell me that I could mentally raise my body temperature, but I can't concentrate on something like that long enough to succeed. And I recently read that a person can get warm by eating calorifacient foods such as chili peppers, but I found they only burn my tongue. A lot of folks feel warm this time of year because even though it's freezing, it's Christmas, a season of giving. And giving is one of the best ways to feel warm and toasty. Isn't it too bad that inward warmth and toastiness can't be transferred outwardly?

Ahh, but it can: by a simple hug. There is something solidly warming about a heartfelt embrace. An honest hug that begins on the inside, ignited in the heart, and then radiates outward through the arms and around can generate a level of warmth that will bring the hugee to the melting point. A loving heart can generate enough warmth to comfort the coldest soul. What a wonderful gift to give or to get.

My hope for everyone is to always have someone within arm's reach.

# In Heart

SEVENTEEN BOTTLES. THAT'S HOW MANY BODY, FACE, AND HAIR PRODUCTS were in my daughter's shower. Although I couldn't read what they were to be used for (because I don't shower with my reading glasses on), I was still able to see well enough to count them. I depend on luck to use the correct bottle for the correct purpose—that's the extent of my gambling endeavors.

My decision to stand among and battle those bottles was really to escape the sickeningly sweet conversation going on in the living room between my daughter and her newlywed, newly deployed husband. He was stationed on an island overseas so she was stationed on her couch as they visited via Skype.

My parents also communicated using technology while my father did his tour of duty in Vietnam, but it was by reel-to-reel tape, not by way of the Internet. Mama did most of the talking, but we kids also sent him messages. On at least one occasion, I used the machine to tattle on my mom. I complained to Papa that Mama was making me wear my cousin's yellow hand-me-down shoes. At first, I really loved those shoes, but when a classmate told a friend that he liked the girl with the yellow shoes, my love for them immediately flip-flopped. (I'll never understand the psychology of that—was it being known as the girl with the yellow shoes or because a boy liked me?) Most likely, by the time my father responded, I had outgrown the shoes and the aversion to being liked by boys. It wasn't the era of instant gratification; we had to wait, and often waiting held the answer.

Another time, my mother lined us six kids up for a photo shoot. She put our backs to the camera, slicked back our hair wetted with the water of Moosehead Lake, then swathed our bodies in beach towels. She sent the picture to my dad with a "who's who" challenge. I asked him if he was able to name us. He was astonished at my wondering and said, "Of course I did; you're my kids."

Just because he wasn't there didn't mean he wasn't there—his heart was. Our bodies and our souls can be in two separate places. Absence of body heat isn't absence of heart because they are with us—just add the *r*.

Looking at those pictures of his children growing up without him, my father must have longed to be home. Our circumstances—good, bad, difficult, or happy—have one common denominator: they are temporary. Eventually Papa returned, and the days were sweet and full.

Do you have a loved one on the other side of the world, the phone line, a computer screen, or eternity? For a lot of us, it still isn't a time of instant gratification. If you, for just a little while, are denied the warm embrace of a loved one, know that person is with you, for he or she is—in heart.

# A Valentine

A VALENTINE ARRIVED THE OTHER DAY, A SEVEN-POUND, THREE-OUNCE bundle of hope. And hopes for her, I have.

I hope she is a beautiful word amid today's flagrant vulgarity and illiteracy. I hope her life is a billet-doux, a love letter to all who come to know her.

I hope she becomes a brilliant amulet.

She is beautiful now—ethereal, even. I hope her beauty continues and increases, not for vanity's sake, for the word *vain* means "empty," but because she is happy—a happy woman is a beautiful woman.

I hope she sees only the nuggets of love niched in the world's walls of hate.

I hope her vocabulary is limited to kind words and truth.

I hope she realizes early in her life that the world can't hurt her if she doesn't want anything from it and can therefore live in freedom from its confines.

I hope this baby rocks. I hope she rocks the world and rocks it so well that she turns it upside down, and everything in it that shouldn't be falls out and shatters against the good, the pure, the perfect.

Most of all, my hope for her is an adventurous, outlandishly outstanding life.

And my word for her is *love*.

So, on these words and these hopes, welcome to the world, lovely little Hattie Mae Murray.

# *Listen*

I CLOSED MY EYES. THE NOISE, THE CHAOS, THE WORRIES OF THE WORLD became dim, then dark, and finally they all went away. Slowly, my hearing became the predominate sense, and I listened.

My infant grandson, Jaxon Rand, was lying on my chest listening to my heartbeat as I listened to his soft, barely audible breathing. He is so new to this world that he has yet to step a foot on it.

My teenage grandson sat nearby. I could hear his deep, husky man chuckle as he listened to a comedian through Internet and earphones. Lying there with my family close, I smiled and thought to myself, "This is contentment. I am so thankful for this. What else is there, out there in the world, with the power to fill my heart so?"

With that question in mind, I asked a long list of friends—friends with vastly different backgrounds, experiences, beliefs, and political convictions—to tell me in one word what they are most thankful for. The top three things are faith, family, and friends. And guess what—it was in that order. (One friend said his pigs, but I put that in the family category.) Nobody said their job, although I know a lot are thankful they have one. Not one person claimed to be thankful for material possessions, social standing, or their accomplishments. These other things have importance, of course, but they don't top the lists because they aren't part of the foundation that a content life is built upon.

Faith, family, and friends have a shared definition: love. That's the answer: love.

Faith is what keeps us upright and moving forward against a world that stands ready to knock us down or discourage us; faith holds us up. That's a mighty strong love. Family is what makes us want to keep going. We do it for them. That's a love that cannot be easily understood or explained—that's how deep it is. Friends are those stalwart souls who stand beside and behind us at the ready, no matter what, so we never face any battle alone. Friendship is the epitome of unselfish love.

Listen for them and then be thankful for those top three things: love, love, and love.

# A Farmer's Field

ON A RECENT DRIVE THROUGH THE COUNTRY, I SAW A MAN STANDING IN his field, pitchfork in hand. He was cultivating his land.

This old farmer didn't have big, expensive, fancy farming equipment—just a pitchfork and a purpose. (It doesn't take fancy to farm; it only takes courage and the willingness to put your hands in the dirt.)

The field was huge, several acres I would guess, but that did not discourage the farmer. His was concentrating on planting one row at a time.

We have each been given a gift, a talent, and a field in which to work. If we don't nurture it, cultivate it, and then share it with others, like this farmer who spends his days and his life toiling in his field and then shares his crops, we have lived a life less than intended.

A life lived less than its purpose is not a life fully lived.

# Talking Turkey

THE SPOILS OF THE 1846 HUNTING TRIP OF A NATIVE AMERICAN AND A colonist were crows and turkeys. When it came time for them to divide the hunt, the colonist tried to take all the turkeys for himself. "You take the crows and I'll take the turkeys, or I'll take the turkeys and you take the crows," he suggested.

Not fooled by this, the Native American replied, "Why you don't talk turkey to me?" In other words, why aren't you being honest?

With that in mind, let's talk turkey about Thanksgiving.

First, where was the first? Elementary school books and modern assumptions teach it was in Plymouth, Massachusetts in 1612, but there are records that indicate other gatherings occurred elsewhere and earlier.

The truth is, thanksgiving celebrations were a common tradition originating in England as a harvest festival. Thanksgivings happened all the time, all over the place, by all sorts of people. Some were celebrations after an extended drought or famine. Some thanksgivings were celebrated after a victory in battle. Many took place upon safe arrival after a dangerous voyage.

Maine claims to be first with a 1606 Popham Beach Thanksgiving when forty-five settlers made landfall there from England.

On December 4, 1619, before the Pilgrims had even departed for the new world, Virginia observed a day of thanksgiving and placed a monument to commemorate it at Berkeley Plantation. That monument reads, "We ordain that this day of our ship's arrival, at a place assigned for plantacon in the land of Virginia shall be yearly and perpetually kept holy as a day of Thanksgiving to Almighty God."

Connecticut celebrated the conclusion of the Pequot War and declared a day of thanksgiving and praise in the month of October.

Even El Paso, Texas claims the fame of hosting the first Thanksgiving. A feast and a day of giving thanks were held in April 1589 after five hundred people survived a brutal expedition across the Chihuahuan Desert to the Rio Grande.

Florida's Spanish explorers claimed to be the first feasters in St. Augustine in September 1565.

Truthfully, the only thing these historic thanksgivings had in common was that they were all acts of giving thanks to God.

The holiday eventually morphed into turkey, stuffing, cranberry sauce, pumpkin pie, naps, and football after it became our national holiday in 1863. President Lincoln, at the urging of Sarah Joseph Hale, who spent twenty years petitioning for it, declared Thanksgiving a holiday as a means of healing our Civil War-torn country. (As you dig into your heaping plate this year, remember to be thankful for a persistent woman!)

Whoever you are, wherever you are from, whatever it is you are celebrating, give thanks, because that's what it's truly all about.

# Being Created a Woman

A GROUP ON A POPULAR SOCIAL MEDIA PAGE PUT FORTH THE QUESTION, "Why are you proud of being a woman?" As a participant of that group, this was my answer: To be created a woman means to be formed from the very bones that protect the heart because a woman's heart is the heart of being a woman. It's where her fire burns—the fire that fuels and illuminates who she is.

"Being created a woman means to possess an inward, quiet strength that brings physical prowess to its knees. It means to be given the freedom to love without reserve and with a fierceness that consumes, yet a tenderness that softens the hardest heart. It means to love with abandon and an absolute entirety.

"Being created a woman means to be blessed by the miracle of birth. Children born from our wombs—by way of our hearts—are then gifted to the world, wrapped in our souls.

"Being created a woman means you see clearly because you see with your heart.

"Being born a woman is a gift from the heart of God.

"I am not proud to be a woman; I am humbled by it."

# The Christmas Gift

MY SIX-YEAR-OLD DAUGHTER KELLY SAVED HER PENNIES, NICKELS, DIMES, and quarters all autumn to buy Christmas gifts for her family. Every coin she found or was given went immediately into her ceramic, pink-flowered, chipped-eared piggy bank. When I watched her pick up a coin from some forgotten spot and purposefully carry it to her bank, I realized, "This is a good thing." So I let her struggle and save. Over the course of three months, she managed to put aside ten dollars.

And then she gave it away.

I don't mean she spent it; I mean she gave it away. The hungry faces of the children in need we all hear about during the holidays tugged at her heart. "Mom, I want to give my money to poor children," she said.

I asked her if she was sure she wanted to do this. She was.

I asked her if she was certain she wanted to give it all. She did.

Her desire to feed the hungry mouths of the children she learned about trumped her desire to see smiles on the faces of her well-fed family as they opened their gifts. Willingly and with much conviction, she handed her money over to feed those kids, expecting nothing in return. Not a flicker of doubt crossed that precious face, not one hint of hesitation could be seen as she gave all her hard-found money to the folks dedicated to feeding the hungry. It was her hand that gave, but it was her heart that propelled.

That very evening our family went to dinner at a local restaurant. As Kelly stepped over a snowbank onto the steps that led into the eatery, she noticed a small triangle of paper sticking out of the snow. She reached down and pulled it out; it was a crumpled, snow-covered twenty-dollar bill.

"If you could have anything you want, what would it be?" asked the eight-year-old daughter of my friend Laura, who was experiencing a devastating Christmas season because of divorce, poverty, and loss.

"Oh, I don't know," sighed Laura. Then, and for no particular reason other than to satisfy her little girl's question, she wished a wish that was as outlandish as the recent turn of events in her life. "I suppose, if the sky were the limit, I'd ask for a diamond and sapphire necklace."

"Then I will pray you get one," promised her child.

A few days before Christmas, mother and child were visiting the family matriarch, Laura's grandmother. Her grandmother left the room and returned carrying a box in her elderly, feeble hands. As she lifted the top, she told Laura, "I'm never going to wear this; I want you to have it." She handed Laura a diamond and sapphire necklace. Laura's eyes widened in stunned amazement and then her jaw dropped when she was handed the matching diamond and sapphire bracelet. Speechless, Laura looked at her daughter who merely smiled sweetly. Before that moment, neither had known the jewelry existed.

The best Christmas gift to be given is the ability to recognize the miracles born of childlike faith.

# The Very Least of These

HE WALKED, SO BENT WITH AGE THAT THE BACK OF HIS JACKET WAS soaked with rain. He did not wear a hat; he did not have gloves; his hands were shoved deep into the pockets of his wet coat. The hems of his pant legs were uneven as if they had been chopped off with whatever implement was close at hand at the time they needed chopping. Those jagged hems were the lines in his story that made me feel sorry for him.

He stood on the corner looking up the street, a confused, thoughtful expression upon his face. He spoke aloud to himself, and although I did not hear his words, his expression made me believe he was wondering if up the street was the way he should go.

He did a better job than I at withstanding the weather, for as he stood under the sleeting skies, I sought shelter in a warm, cozy book-store, but I quickly found a window to continue watching him. (How often do we do that—stand in a place of comfort and watch those who may be struggling?)

He crossed the street and wandered up the sidewalk, away, out of sight, but not out of mind, for I could not stop thinking about him. I wondered, what was his story? Was he needy, poor, hungry? Worse than those, was he lonely? Should I have spoken to him? Should I have bought him a hot cup of tea? Should I have offered him a ride? Should I have asked him if there was something I could do for him? I wish I could now say "I did…" instead of "I should have…"

Some would say, "Leave him alone; he's sleeping in the bed he made." So what if he was? Aren't beds made to get messy? You can always remake a bed.

Perhaps I am misguided in all this. Maybe he was merely ec-centric, and it's arrogant of me to think he needed anything from me. I don't have enough fingers and toes to count the times I've gone out inappropriately dressed. I've made a quick run to the market in torn SpongeBob boxer shorts. I often talk to myself (with hand gestures, even!). I have the worst sense of direction, so I'm often wondering where I am. I've been accused of being eccentric.

Maybe he's just like me. Maybe he was fine.

And maybe he wasn't.

I should have stepped out of that warm, dry bookstore—out of my comfort zone—and gone where he was and asked. Instead, I watched him walk out of sight. (I think there are many, many people in need, living out of sight.)

I want everyone to feel love, even if just for a moment. I don't want anyone—especially our elderly—to have to stand alone on the corner in the freezing rain, wondering where they are.

That day, I didn't do what I should have done. No matter what this man's story, the very least I should have done was put my hand on his, smiled at him, and asked.

# Once Upon A Time

ONCE UPON A TIME, NOT THAT MANY GENERATIONS AGO, WHEN LIFE IN Maine was tough and so were the people, there lived a little girl. Her name was Delia. Delia lived in southern Aroostook County in the late 1800s. In those days, children were only as secure as their parent's health, and Delia had a happy, safe childhood until her mother died of tuberculosis. Her grandparents, unable to care for her, sent her out to find work with only a bundle of clothing tucked under her arm. She was nine years old. It wasn't that her grandparents didn't want or love Delia, it's just that they were poor sheep farmers, and it took all they had to keep her younger brother. Their poverty wasn't a sign of the times, it was the times. Delia wrote in her memoir, "I started out walking, carrying my bundle, hungry, not a cent of money."

People took her in and she found work as a cook, laundress, housekeeper, and child-care provider. She was even a farm hand— she shoveled hay until she fainted from exhaustion or picked barrels and barrels of potatoes until it seemed her back would break. She wrote, "I didn't earn enough to pay for the clothes I wore out."

Some homes were kindly, but many were not. Delia was often mistreated, battered, assaulted, neglected, or used as slave labor. On one occasion, a "rough and crude" man (as she described him) abused Delia and spit tobacco juice in her eye. (While researching Delia's life and visiting the areas where she grew up, I came across the headstone of this man. Remembering his penchant for spitting on people, I wanted to spit on his grave, but knowing where he is now and that he would relish moisture in any form, I refrained.)

On another occasion, because the woman of the house didn't think Delia heated the dishwater enough, she held Delia's hands in steaming hot water until she screamed.

These are only a couple of examples of the torment this little girl endured for nine long years. Delia spent many days frightened, hungry, exhausted, and lonely. As I read her memoirs I realized that through it all, even on those days she prayed to die, there remained a tiny spark of something that kept her going. She dreamed of her future and how things would be different. She thought of the ways she would treat her own children. She comforted herself with simple things that brought her pleasure, like the rag doll she treasured or eating strawberries found in a field. That tiny spark was hope—the belief and trust that one's desires can be had, or that events will turn out for the best.

No matter what Delia endured, she looked to better days. Hope—this strange and powerful thing exclusive to the human race—helped her survive terrible circumstances. I wonder where her hope came from. Maybe, having been stripped of all else, it was the only thing left, so she clung to it, cherished it, and fostered it. It, in turn, saved her.

Time passed and Delia grew to adulthood and became the loving, nurturing mother of eight children. I am thankful she held on to her hope for a brighter future, for if Delia had given up on life, my life would have been given up as well because she was my great-grandmother.

# *What Is Love?*

LOVE IS ALL-CONSUMING, COMPLICATED, MESSY. IT DEFINES DAYS, mediates nights, and engulfs souls. These things need not be true, for love need not be extravagant.

In its most basic definition, love is the call to take care of one another. "Take care of one another"—a contradiction in terms! For "to take" is a selfish action; it means to touch, to grasp in order to bring something to oneself.

When we answer the call to take care of one another, we touch, we grasp, we bring to ourselves a life lived in the fullness of love's true meaning.

# Let Them Eat Cake

I DON'T EAT CAKE. ITS SUGAR MESSES UP MY SUGAR—MY BLOOD SUGAR surges, then crashes. I don't hate the way cake tastes, I hate the way it feels.

I don't eat a lot of chocolate; large amounts gives me heartburn. So cake with chocolate icing, for me, is a double whammy.

The cake was chocolate with pink M&M's on the top. Gooey and moist and delicious-looking.

"I brought you a piece of cake!"

My heart melted like the cake's icing, which was dripping down his four-year-old hand.

"You did? Thank you so much! Why did you bring me a piece of cake?"

"Because you love cake," he said.

And yes, it was delicious. And yes, I ate every bite.

This is how far you should go for someone you love: with an outstretched hand, opened with a pure, simple childlike offering in faith.

PART FOUR

*"A friend knows the song
in my heart and sings it to me
when my memory fails."*

——DONNA ROBERTS

# Brave Girls

I WASN'T VERY BIG WHEN I WAS LITTLE. BUT I WAS BRAVE, AND THAT bravery made up for my shortcomings.

When my first day of kindergarten was over, I walked home. The problem with that is I didn't know the way, only I didn't know I didn't know the way—I just opened the schoolhouse door and started walking, absolutely certain I would find my way home.

After searching all afternoon, my parents finally found me at dusk wandering the sidewalks. I do not remember feeling afraid (which may be a reflection not of being daring, but of being dumb). It's only as an adult and a mother that I think back and imagine how frantic my parents must have felt. I was supposed to wait for my older brother who, from practice the year before, knew the way home.

Some of my female friends are brave souls, too. A few weeks ago I called a friend on her cell phone and asked, "Where are you?"

"On top of Spaulding Mountain," she said.

"But we're in the middle of a snowstorm!" I said.

"Yes, I know, and I'm really cold," she said.

"And it's dark!" I added.

"Yeah, I know that too, but it's okay; I'm staying the night. There's a lean-to up here. There's also another hiker."

"Oh, good," I said. "Well, at least you're not alone." My sarcasm could have melted the snow on several mountains.

I have other friends who don't think there is an ounce of bravery in them. One such friend didn't feel she could walk her woodland road for fear of the aggressive dogs that live near her. Each time she tried to take her pup for a stroll, those untamed beasts would threaten them. She asked me for help.

"It's not the dogs; it's the owner," we both said, but since the owner refused to listen to my friend's pleas to control his pets, I decided to talk to the dogs—so off we set, shaking in our boots, but walking tall and carrying a big stick. When we reached the end of the neighbor's driveway, the expected attack came: two huge, frightening, growling and barking animals charged us with fangs and fury showing. I stood firm (truth be known, probably more frozen from fear than bravado). And so, in for a penny, in for a pound of my flesh, I raised my stick and with a loud, commanding voice screamed, "Noooooo!"

The dogs skidded to a halt.

"Git!" I yelled at them again. (A little successful courage breeds more.)

The dogs retreated—all the way back up the driveway and around the corner, out of sight. My friend who claimed to be too afraid to do this on her own is more courageous than she thinks because asking for help is one of the scariest things of all. It is often viewed as a sign of weakness, but is in fact a true act of bravery.

But by far, the bravest girls I know are those who have gathered up their courage and left bad situations. Those girls have stepped out into the unknown—alone or with the help of a friend, perhaps in fear, yet carrying the big stick of belief that it will be a better, safer, happier, healthier life for them.

Kudos to brave girls.

# *Just for Fun*

THE OTHER DAY, A DAY FULL OF BUSINESS COMMITMENTS, ERRANDS, chores, parents, children, and grandchildren, my friend Laura and I decided to veer off our course of responsibility to go for a hike and do some shopping. Not that we are rebellious (okay, I admit I am, but only in a good way), it's just that there are those sunny spring days when the gentle breezes whisper our names and the boughs of the pines wave a beckoning call—a seductive song that silences our serious side, and we just can't handle being responsible for one moment longer. This was just such a day, and it turned into a day just for fun.

As we approached the trailhead we came across a guy in a field. He was lounging in a lawn chair in front of a helicopter.

Our necks slowly craned around to better view the odd sight as we drove past.

Laura stopped the car and looked at me. I read her mind. "We have to know, don't we?" I asked.

She nodded and backed up the vehicle. "Whose helicopter is that?" she called from her window.

"I was sitting here wondering the same thing," the guy said. We laughed.

She defended us, "Well, we're going for a hike, and we wondered if maybe you were looking for a bad guy out loose in the woods and we should know where he is."

I was impressed with her quickness of mind to think of that excuse. "Wow," I whispered.

"And if he's a good-looking bad guy, you want to know exactly where he is." Lawn-Chair Man's mind was as quick as Laura's. We laughed again.

We eventually found out that it was indeed his helicopter and he was—like us—taking a break from working—he, on a mountain-top tower somewhere close by.

The helicopter was still in the field when we returned, although Lawn-Chair Man was gone. Again, we stopped. I can't explain why, except it's a helicopter in the middle of a field in the middle of nowhere and we needed to look at it some more. As we sat there looking, a car pulled up beside us. It was two lost young men.

"Do you know where Tumbledown Mountain is?" one asked Laura.

"Yes," Laura said, then fell silent, lost in thought.

She evidently took too much time to think, and the fellow impatiently asked, "Well, would you mind telling me where?"

Laura is one of the sweetest, most giving people I know, but she didn't appreciate being rushed as she tried to mentally map the best route for him, so she pointed across the valley at the mountain range to our east and answered, "It's over there."

We spent the rest of our day shopping in our favorite stores: farm supply shops, garden centers, and greenhouses. At the farm store, Laura was trying to pet a goldfish at the koi display while I was trying not to gag at the collection of pet rodents for sale. One such pet rodent (a contradiction in terms if I ever heard one) had a sign on its cage that read: "This little guy will not bite you, but he will try to lick you with his very sharp teeth." My burst of laughter caused Laura to abandon her fishing and join me.

It is now days later and I am back to work, but the memory of the two of us standing at that pet display, laughing, still brings a smile to my face.

I am so thankful that I have friends and days made just for fun.

# Women on the Move

## Because I Wanted To

The conversation about travel began when I told a group of friends about my desire to own a railroad caboose to haul behind my Jeep. While on the topic of train travels, one of the women told us of her solo train trip across Canada and her lengthy tour of Alaska, a brave thing for a middle-aged woman to do alone. I was amazed at her audacity and fearlessness to undertake such a wandering.

"Whatever made you do such a thing?" I asked her.

"Because I wanted to," she said. This is all the explanation a truly free spirit ever needs.

## Because I Can

I was joking with two female acquaintances about my recent redonning of my motorcycle gear. This gear had been stored in the back of my closet for almost fifteen years.

"I've dusted off my Harley boots and my carefree ways, and now I'm back on the back of a motorcycle!" I told them. "My daughters are wondering what's going on with me these days. They think I've lost my marbles and misplaced my maturity!"

The ladies gave one another a look, and then turned to look at me.

"I imagine a motorcycle is loads of fun," Judith said. "I captain and navigate a thirty-six-foot yacht from Cape Cod to Florida and back several times a season."

Louise piped in, "And I pilot my own Piper Warrior airplane."

(The modes of transportation these ladies choose sort of makes travel by a motorcycle seem as easy as riding a bike.)

Louise went on to explain how after taking one lesson, she fell in love with flying and became a pilot. Her husband stood behind her, silently and slowly nodding his head. His expression of surrender spoke more than words could ever express. I could imagine his thoughts—they said it all: "What are you going to do? Give up and die? Or give up and let her live?"

## Because I Am Free

I am going to my grandson's birthday party this weekend—a super-hero-themed party, and all those invited are asked to dress as their favorite superhero.

After much consideration, I have decided to go as Grandmother. Grandmothers are often incredible superheroes. I am going to wear my granny sweater, the top button fastened at my neck, and as I drive to the party with the Jeep top down it will wave in the wind behind me like a cape. I have a lead foot, but this time when I am pulled over, I can say to the policeman, "Yes, officer, I know how fast I was going—I was flying."

# The Month Before Christmas

'Twas the month before Christmas,
and everyone I know
was rushing around;
it's really quite a show.
All in a hurry
to make everything right
for that special day
and that special night.
I met a friend for a quick cup of joe;
she was hurried and had places to go.
Most of the garland
you see around town
was made by her hands—
she hardly sits down.
I too was busy with so much to do,
all Christmas-related; what else is new?
We stopped for a moment
because we're dear friends.
She pulled up a chair
and parked her rear end.
We had a speed friendship,
our mouths and hands flapping.
We really took off
with our hasty up-catching.
She turned to me,
a smile on her face,
and called a reminder
as she departed the place,
"Remember to breathe!
And remember to smile!
This crazy life lasts just a short while."

Then she was off
like a wee busy bee
to serve the hungry
and people in need.
Then there's my friend
with a too-busy mind
in the middle of talking
a thought came—ill-timed.
She looked at her legs
and said to the floor,
"Remember: buy eggs,
you don't have anymore."
(Her to-do list so squeezed
that she talks to her knees.)
Another friend warned,
"L.E., stay warm."
"Don't worry," I said,
"Relax and calm down.
I'm moving so fast,
I could heat the whole town!"
The lights and the tinsel,
the tree and the food,
the presents, the people,
the singing, the mood…
Christmas is coming,
it's looming,
it's near!
Is everything perfect?
(Unlike last year.)
We must make it so,
that's why we're this busy!
Just one thing awry
puts us right in a tizzy.

It's important, you see,
we must make it merry!
All I want for Christmas
is January.

# *Growing Gardener*

---

I<small>T</small> <small>WAS MY INTENTION TO TAKE THE BOTTLES TO THE REDEMPTION</small> center, meet my friends Laura and Lauren for lunch, and then come home. I did the first two things and eventually the last, but it took me ten hours. You see, it's time to put in the gardens, and my friends are gardeners—good ones—and are actually paid to garden. They are certified professionals, and they work in the field in which they excel: the field. They feed by growing fruits and vegetables and by educating the public. They save heirloom variety seeds and therefore save future gardens and gardeners—they do that because they are smart gardeners.

I needed cucumbers because my plants died. (I am obviously not a professional. I recently found out I don't even know how to hill potatoes correctly.) So, when they invited me to go with them for the afternoon, I accepted. I sat in the backseat, listening to them talk about their work. I leaned forward slightly left or right, allowing any tidbit of valuable information that wafted back toward me to fully envelop and educate me, like a thirsty flower leans toward a drop of rain, ever hopeful.

I have no idea where we went as we hopscotched across western Maine, but we visited some of the state's finest greenhouses, farms, and gardens. Laura and Lauren know exactly where these places are because they are gardeners au courant.

One of the greenhouses was on a hill with a fantastic view of the mountains. If there is one thing that can turn my gaze from flowers, that is it. In awe, I blurted out to the proprietor, "Have you seen this view?" (Of course he had.) He held his hands out, palms up, and looked at me like I was a potato head.

Another greenhouse/garden was devoted to a seed-saver program, and while my friend Lauren spoke with the farmer (technically he was a curator of seeds), I wandered from plant to plant like an insect, fascinated with the place, continually asking, "What is that?

What is that?" There was stuff growing everywhere—acres and acres—on purpose!

The farmer, Lauren, and Laura talked the talk of highly educated growers as they walked the walkways of the vast farm, stopping at a bed to discuss varieties, then looking over a field and talking about techniques. They did that because they are dedicated gardeners. I followed behind, daydreaming.

As the end of our visit neared, the farmer made wooden markers for the selection of plants that were to go with Lauren. I asked if I could help. He handed me some cedar plant markers and said, "You are ornamental." He then trotted back up to the house for a pen.

I turned to Lauren and Laura. "What do you suppose he means?"

Lauren said, "Maybe he thinks you're pretty."

I scoffed, "I highly doubt that! More likely he thinks I'm useless."

Laura ended the debate and with a laugh said, "Perhaps he thinks you're pretty useless."

Our final stop before going to our respective homes (and gardens) was the ice-cream shop. With cone in hand we naturally strolled toward the flower bed there. I leaned over and pulled a weed or two. I did that because my friends are patient with me, water me well, and enrich my life; therefore I'm a growing gardener.

# The Story of Harry

I said I wasn't going to do this. I said I would not write about my dog, but then again, I said I wouldn't have a dog. I didn't really want a dog. I'm a cat person.

But here is the story of Harry.

I accompanied my pet-seeking friend to the animal shelter, simply to accompany my best friend. I had no intention of adopting a different best friend. Once there, I was invited to fill out an adoption form and so I did, because I didn't have anything else to do while I waited.

The form invited me to list the attributes of a dog I might be interested in adopting. I knew there was no such dog under creation that would meet all my requirements, so I gladly submitted the form with the following demands:

A small dog only.

Not a puppy, because I don't have time to train it.

Not an old dog, because I don't want to fall in love and then lose it.

It has to be a hypoallergenic non-shedder.

It has to like babies and small children because my daughters have those.

It has to like other dogs because my daughters have those, too.

I will accept the following breeds: (Yes, I actually stated this.)

Coton de Tulear

Bichon Frise

Havenese

No yippy dogs.

NO POODLES. (Sorry, poodle people.)

I handed the paper in and smugly said, "Here." To myself I snickered and said, "There! Good luck finding that dog!"

Two days later my phone rang. "We found your dog," they said.

"You're kidding." I couldn't believe it.

"We found Harry in North Carolina, and Pilots for Paws flew down and brought him back to Maine."

"You're kidding," I repeated.

"No, we're not kidding," they assured me. "Harry was a stray, abandoned, and on the list to be euthanized."

"You're kidding! That's terrible!" I said.

"Come meet him," they invited.

So I met Harry, a small, hypoallergenic non-shedder, kid- and pet-friendly, four-year-old Bichon Frise mix that doesn't bark much (much less yip). Within the first minute of our introduction, he hopped onto my lap and settled in—as if that was where he belonged. And that is exactly how it felt—as if he belonged there.

I looked into his sad eyes and said, "Okay, I'll rescue you."

I didn't want a dog, but Harry is not doglike. He's more like a cat, or one of those Hollywood dogs. He's fluffy. He fits in my purse. My two-year-old grandson knows the difference between dogs and cats (because he has one of each), and he points at Harry and says, "Kitty?" If Harry is humiliated he doesn't show it, probably because he is so pampered. His dog food and bank biscuits are softened with chicken broth. He gets fed before I do; he goes to the beautician and manicurist more often than I do. But he earns his keep by keeping my feet warm—and by being the absolute best, most loyal buddy ever.

Yes, he's perfect for me, this cat-dog, even though that "mix" part I mentioned earlier…is most assuredly poodle.

## PART FIVE

*"When you arise in the morning, think of what a precious privilege it is to be alive— to breathe, to think, to enjoy, to love."*

—MARCUS AURELIUS

# After the Storm

I WAS EXPLAINING TO A FRIEND MY CHOICE FOR THE COVER PHOTO OF MY last book, *Diamonds from the Corner.* It's a picture of a young girl drinking the raindrops that are falling on her. I explained, "The raindrops represent our life stories, some good, some not so good. We can't stop the rain—we can't always stop what comes at us in life—so we might as well drink it in and hope some good will come of it."

She thought about that for a moment, then said, "I think instead of an image of a sweet child enjoying the raindrops, the picture should be of a woman in a hailstorm with bandages on her head."

"I concur!" concurred another friend.

Obviously those two were experiencing challenging weeks.

We all have trying times. Life can be storm-ridden and difficult. We fail, our kids fail, we lose jobs, we lose friends, our bodies break down, and then so does the car. Just when you don't think you can handle one more thing, one more thing happens. The sorrows and problems of this world are as varied as the people in it and as numerous as raindrops. We all, at one time or another, get left out in the rain, where it's wet, miserable, and cold.

Storm waters are sometimes easily maneuvered, but often it takes all our treading powers to stay afloat as we watch the things around us swirl away and disappear downriver. The good news is, storms end, and after the storm, the sky clears and the rebuilding can start. All that stuff that washed away was one of two things: debris that needed to go, or something that needed to be replaced with something bigger, better, and stronger. After you weather your dark days successfully, you are then able to help others weather theirs. And in doing so, you realize that trials don't necessarily make raindrops taste sweeter, but they are certainly more palatable. The rain watered you so you could grow. It cleaned the bugs off your windshield. Now you are qualified to remind the newly drenched that the sun is out there, and it will return.

I remember the day my niece, a very small child at the time, fell into the lake. She kicked and splashed and cried out in a panic, "Help me! I'm drowning, I'm drooooowwwnnning!"

"Stand up!" her mother yelled to her from shore.

When she bravely stood, she could see the waters that had threatened to overwhelm her and take away her life were only ankle-deep.

Perhaps we should learn to boldly stand up when we feel we are going under. Then maybe we'd see the water for what it really is: not something intended to kill us, but rather something we are able to wade through.

# Out of the Ordinary

I WAS AT THE GARAGE, DOING AN ORDINARY THING: WAITING FOR MY TIRES to be rotated. While I waited, I watched the mechanic work on my car through the waiting-room window. Not that I'm interested in that sort of thing, it's just that I was less interested in what the other customers were watching on the television, which was so unmemorable that I can't name it here.

A man approached and put his face to the window, a mere inch from my face. He made me jump when he loudly asked, "Are they finished?" His nearness alarmed me, and I took a step backward. He then began a one-sided monologue that continued, with barely a breath inhaled, for well over ten minutes.

I reminded myself to be kind, to be gracious, because I read that sometimes we entertain angels unaware, so we should be kind to strangers just in case. As his monologue lengthened, I ditched my convictions and thought, "Is this an angel or an idiot?"

At the very moment I had that thought, the man spoke again. "Is that your Wrangler? I used to have a Wrangler, but this happened." He lifted the hair covering his forehead and showed me a very large U-shaped scar on his forehead.

"Oh, gawd, Lew-Ellyn!" I admonished myself. "You just labeled a possibly brain-injured person an idiot, you idiot!" Then I thought it was probably worse of me to judge him based on a scar than on a penchant for incessant chatter. That, in truth, I shouldn't judge him on either of those things—or on anything at all.

In trying to keep up with his rant, my thoughts couldn't catch up with themselves to decide what to think of this guy, so I stood still in a stunned silence and simply stared at him.

He went on to tell me he wasn't "Jeeping" when his accident happened twenty-five years ago. He was on his way home from work, just a mile from home, when his Jeep veered off the road and cartwheeled. He was in a coma for eleven days, and while he was in the coma his son was born. He thinks he knew that, and that is what brought him back to consciousness. For that reason, he has always called his son his hero.

He said he now drives a truck and his life purpose is to spread discontent, and then he smiled in such a broad, mischievous way that I wasn't sure if he was kidding or proving his point.

Without warning he veered off the subject, much like his Jeep must have swerved off the road all those years ago. "So, what do you do for entertainment?" he wanted to know. I was completely adrift in this heavily one-sided encounter and was left without wit or wisdom. I opened my mouth and shut it again—twice, which was not to imply I fish for entertainment. He didn't wait for me to answer. Just as suddenly as he appeared, he was gone. As I watched him walk away, still talking to himself about needing onions and paper towels, I thought, "Wow, that was out of the ordinary."

"We meet no ordinary people in our lives." —C.S. Lewis

# *A Higher Education*

THERE WAS A BLACK GIRL SITTING ON THE BLEACHERS IN HER SCHOOL-assigned, one-piece, periwinkle-blue gym suit with cuffs rolled at the knees. While she waited for gym class to begin, she ate pickled pigs' feet from a jar filled with a murky liquid of water, pork fat, and spices. A white girl sat there, too; she was eating from a box of assorted powdered donuts. Later that day I told my mother about the girl. I wasn't allowed to eat donuts, so I wanted her to know people eat them and survive.

"She eats donuts every day," I confided.

"Well, she must be a chunk!" My mother was always on the alert for any chunky habits I might pick up.

"She's not a chunk; she's skinny!" I said.

"Then she doesn't eat donuts every day. Anyone who eats do-nuts every day has to be a chunk." This was the last word—Mama's, of course.

Papa had only one rule. "When in Rome, do as the Romans do." This is why I was bused from my home on the military base in Charleston, South Carolina, to an inner-city, previously all-black high school during the desegregation of the southern school systems. It wasn't the original desegregation (I'm not that old!), it was the sec-ondary integration of schools naturally segregated by neighborhoods.

The bus ride through the city was long and confining. I would lean my head against the window, close my eyes, and let my mind go. After watching my ritual for a few weeks, a bus mate brought me a small travel pillow, "So your nap will be more comfortable," he said. I took the offering, but explained, "I'm not sleeping; I'm dreaming." Back then, I'd rather dream than be instructed, so not a lot of study-ing took place. And although I don't remember opening my school books (I opened library books instead), I remember lugging them. High school was a heavy burden in turbulent times. I was a poor stu-dent, but I learned a lot.

The foreign language on my class list was Spanish, but my everyday language lessons were in Ebonics and the unique dialect of the poor white kids with thick southern accents. The speech of some of my teachers was just as thick. My math teacher told the class to draw a lion. My hand froze in confusion. "What do you mean, 'draw a lion'?"

"Not a *lion*, child, a *lion*…from point A to point B…a lion!" she drawled.

And of course, there were the colors to cope with.

My mother told me because of my olive-colored skin, wearing green clothes made me look seasick and I should avoid that shade. My friend was told by her mother that she shouldn't wear solid yellow. "What's the matter with yellow?" I wanted to know.

"Mother said with my black skin, I look like a bee."

We were typical teenager girls, trying to find our personal style; that was the extent of our concern for colors.

Many days were fearful. There were riots and vandalism. My bus was turned over, and I remember feeling indignant about that. There were cops and gangs and grumblings. There was a shooting in the parking lot. I found out later that the authors of the chaos were malcontents from elsewhere. Why were they afraid that this melding would succeed? If I'd had the presence of mind, I would have stood up and yelled, "Get your mess out of our halls!" But I was more concerned with getting my presence in front of the cute boys and away from the science teacher, who was solely responsible for helping me perfect my eye-rolling technique.

Some of the trouble was caused by parents who thought their children deserved more. More of what, I don't know. I couldn't have enjoyed the things I saw any more than I did—like the styling guy with goldfish swimming in the glass heels of his boots or the two girls fistfighting in the hallway, one minus her halter top that had been ripped off by her foe.

Many wanted their children in a different environment. I can't imagine an atmosphere any more different than one with so many social classes attending the same high-school classes. Perhaps they thought being around people so strangely different would cause their kids to become different from them. They were right; it did. It made us kids blind to those differences. We were in the corner, giggling and wondering if the new boy in math class had a girlfriend. We were talking about clothes, music, the mall, and how the snobby, pretty captain of the cheerleading team was expecting a baby with the studly captain of the football team, and we were all secretly tickled that she was getting fat.

Yes, we were—we are—different. Some of us liked pickled pigs' feet, some of us liked donuts. Some of us had black skin, some had white, and some, like me, had olive. We spoke different languages; we believed different things. And yet, we were all alike: kids in a wanton world, just trying to be kids. And since kids will always be kids, no matter what adults think or do, we succeeded.

# *Un-Fair*

"CAROLINE! CAROLINE! DO NOT WALK AWAY FROM ME. WE ARE NOT getting ice cream!" His boom-box voice sounded miserly and mean. I looked around for Caroline and recognized her immediately. She was standing a dozen feet away from Mr. Boombox, her stiffened back facing him—he was the obvious group leader. Her arms and countenance were crossed; her chin and convictions raised high. She clutched a sweater in those crossed arms as if it were her only comfort, a security blanket for a kid on the edge of the adult world. I guessed she was the age of independent thinking, but not independence.

I'm a kid; I'm at a fair; I want an ice cream.

She was standing still, which qualified her as being obedient for not walking away, yet her turned back was her assertion as she stood against the powers that be.

I did not know the details, and there may have been a legitimate reason for denying her, but I could not justify one. A kid at a fair should be allowed ice cream.

As I approached this skinny little Joan of Arc, I sensed something about her; her small stature standing firm in the massive crowd made her stand out.

There was strength in how tightly she clutched that sweater.

There was courage in her rigidity.

Her silent steadfastness spoke to me: she was not being a brat, and this was not about ice cream. Although her feet stood still, she was taking a first step in asserting her hardwired instinct to stand up for her right to take control of her own life.

And then I knew why she was being denied such a seemingly small thing as an ice-cream cone—to give her practice for the years ahead. It takes practice to take control of something as complex and unruly as life.

My heart rooted for this child—this child that the rest of the world might, at first glance and misunderstanding, define as a hard-headed, spoiled, determined, badly behaved brat.

It's a fair, she's a kid, give her an ice cream.

I knew—everyone knew—she was going to breathe out, turn around, rejoin her group, go without, obey…she would give in this time (when she was ready), but she will never give up her rights.

I walked into her peripheral vision. The only body parts she allowed to move were her red-hot fiery eyes as she gave me a sideward glance. Our eyes met. Her mouth was set in stone. My mouth is now old and wrinkled from years of saying "I do not accept your rules for my life."

I had one more thing to say about this, and it was to her. "I love you," I mouthed.

# On Bikes and Bugs and Being Tough

I SWALLOWED A BUG. YOU'VE HEARD IT SAID IT'S WISE TO KEEP YOUR mouth shut—that is true and doubly so when mountain biking. This bug wasn't a no-see-um; I definitely saw it coming straight at me, but we were both going too fast to avoid the incident. There was nothing I could do except gag, which I did, at length and with purpose.

It tasted like insect hair and antennae. (Excuse me a moment while I stop writing and gag some more.)

When I go out on my bike, I expect to get muddy and beat up; I expect to be cold, hot, sweaty, and exhausted. I even expect to crash on occasion. I accept all those things, but just because I'm in the bugs' world does not mean I accept the bug life into mine—especially on such intimate terms.

When I was a child, my father ate bugs. He would pick one up, make sure I was watching, and with a mischievous grin pop it in his mouth. He made a theatrical production of chewing and swallowing, then would end by smacking his lips and saying something disgusting like, "Yum!" He would answer my horrified little-girl expression, complete with bug eyes and mouth agape, with, "What? It's protein!"

(If I want protein, I'll eat a moose.)

As I think back on those times and my father's teasing grin, I remember he only ate creepy crawlers while I was present and watching. This makes me suspicious now. I don't think he actually ate those bugs. I think he used sleight of hand to make me believe he did.

I think he was trying to make a man out of me.

Although he survived jungle survival training for the military, perhaps in part by partaking of those mealy meals, I wonder now if he really ate crispy critters in front of me when he didn't have to. I wonder. I'll never know.

When we biked together—and we often did—he would frown if I used the easy gears. He never let me use the low gears on the hills, even the steep ones. He said, "You can't build muscle if you always take the easy way. One day you're going to need muscle," he'd say.

I once hit a woodland bridge hidden by some tall grass. My biked stopped abruptly, but I did not. I landed upside down in the pucker brush and water. He peddled past, and without any parental concern or even a glance in my direction, said, "I'm glad that wasn't me. That would have hurt me."

I think he was trying to toughen me up.

I picked myself up, dusted myself off, got back on the bike (quite upset and vocal), and worked to catch up to my dad. Eventually I did.

His training worked; I'm tough enough now. I've climbed a whole bunch of challenging hills; I've earned my muscle. I'll never be a man, but I am finally like him. I ate a bug—a bigger, badder, nastier, and more grotesquely gnarly bug than any he ever ate.

And I really ate it.

# *My Vacation*

---

I'M STAYING IN A LITTLE PLACE IN THE BIG WOODS, FAR AWAY AND immensely different from my home. It's quiet here; it's peaceful; it's heavenly, although the noise of an occasional aircraft overhead reminds me I'm still on earth.

I've left my bed and breakfast, where oodles of guests stay, to be a guest in someone else's home for a few days. The homeowners aren't here; they are on their own vacation in Tennessee, at someone else's home. It's sort of like Airbnb, that online marketplace that connects people looking to rent their homes or looking to rent a getaway home for themselves. It's a great way to experience a bit of another person's world. As the owner of a B&B, I experience bits of the lives of others for a living. I like that.

This is my first morning here, and the second thing I have to do is nothing (coffee at dawn on the deck was first). That's the exact opposite of what I do at home. At home, I am up at dawn to begin a day that often, in the busy season, ends sixteen hours later. I don't mind hard work—it has a reward—although at times my lack of sleep comes back to haunt me, like the time I tried to pay the Hannaford cashier with a Mobil gas card. (I dared her with my glare to speak what I knew she was thinking. She wisely held her tongue.)

One reward of running a B&B is getting a taste of the world through the lives of others, their stories, experiences, and life choices, without leaving my home. There is nothing more interesting than another human being—we are such a queer species, and that fascinates me. I learn something new about the world and the people in it every single time someone walks through my door—be it for a moment or a month.

Just this week a geographical historian/professor who has hiked the Appalachian Trail ten times to document the changes in the landscape was here. (And I thought my job was exhausting!) I heard all the trail tales about the personalities and situations that incite drama or comedy. They were great stories that made me laugh.

Another guest, a New York City bus driver with a north Jersey accent, gave me his account of the terrorist attacks on the twin towers. He was there, and his descriptive retelling made me feel as if I were, too. He brought a human touch to the television coverage that I watched that horrible day.

Most recently (the day I left, actually), I hosted a retired ATF agent who is now wandering the country until she falls in love with a hometown and a home. She's not homeless, she just hasn't found one yet. She thinks maybe a place in Monson might be hers because the kitchen has a red floor. Those are the details that fascinate me and make me fall in love with people and their idiosyncrasies. I love it when people share their lives with me.

I'd better get busy at my own vacation. I've got things to see, places to explore, adventures to have. Later, there will be a gathering with friends, old and new. We'll learn a little (or a whole bunch) more about one another's lives, and therefore broaden our own as we share our stories. And of course we will laugh and love our time together.

Just like home.

## Days I Don't Want to Be Me

---

IT WOULD HAVE BEEN KINDER TO HUMANITY IF I HAD STAYED HOME; THAT was the degree of my distraction. But I needed to eat, so I allowed my preoccupied self to go to the store.

When I arrived, I grabbed my car keys and a ten-dollar bill. There was no need to take my purse into the grocery since I was simply getting a couple items, which also made using a cart or basket unnecessary.

After a lengthy deliberation at the peach bin, I finally chose two, grabbed a protein drink, and hurried to the checkout where I dropped everything on the moving conveyer belt.

My ten-dollar bill disappeared. "Oh, frick!" I said to myself. To the cashier, I said, "I think my ten-dollar bill went in there." I pointed to the space at the end of the belt that leads to the nether land under the counter.

Her head dropped a little to the side, and her expression fell a bit, too. "I'll have to call someone." Her tone reminded me of those times my mother warned a misbehaving me, "I'll have to call your father." (Thank God this wasn't my local market where the folks know me.)

To the people in line behind me, she said, "You all might want to change to another register." There were a lot of sighs and shaking heads as they followed her instructions.

Let me state right here, the cashier was trying to be gracious, and she was absolutely kind, but I had disrupted her line, her routine, and understandably, her patience.

She called the manager, who surveyed the situation, then sighed deeply and called another manager who stood, hands on hips, lips pursed, starring at the chore before him. After his own lengthy de-liberation, he took action. He lifted the silver guard that covered the belt where it disappeared under the counter. The only thing in that space was a little package of picante sauce, the type that comes with a take-out meal. (He replaced the cover without removing the picante, which seemed strange to me, but of course, I reminded myself, he had other things on his mind besides getting rid of trash—foremostly, getting rid of me.)

He next removed a tray from somewhere under the counter on the cashier's side. The stuff in the tray was incredibly nasty, but surprisingly colorful—pink, green, orange, red, and yellow bits of food and package pieces, but alas, the only money was a lone penny. Then, he walked around to my side of the counter and painstakingly removed a sizable door that was screwed in place. The cavity under the counter and conveyer belt was revealed. It held oodles of dirt and dust, but no dollars.

"I don't know what to tell you," he shrugged.

"Well, I appreciate you taking all this time and effort to look," I said. To the cashier, I added, "I'll be right back with more money."

On my way out the door, I noticed my crumpled ten-dollar bill on the floor in front of the peach bin. Oops.

Are you wondering what had me so distracted? I was puzzled over what to write about this week.

# What Is Old?

SHE TOLD ME I HAD LOVELY SHOULDERS. NOT SUCH AN ODD THING TO say, except we had just met. It could be that she, being in her late eighties, had decided she didn't have a whole lot of reason to keep her thoughts to herself anymore, especially if those thoughts were the kind and generous sort.

I told her that her eyes were captivating. And they were; they sparkled. She had the eyes of a kindhearted, unselfish woman. A woman who freely compliments another woman and does not feel she has diminished her own worth by doing so.

She said, "Well, isn't it nice for us to sit here and admire one another?" Without waiting for me to agree, she added, "You must be waiting for Sarah."

I was indeed waiting for my great-aunt Sarah to emerge from the nursing home bathroom. After nearly a half hour of waiting, I tapped on the bathroom door. "Sarah? Are you going to be much longer?" I asked.

"What is it to you if I'm in here all day?" she snapped. I guess Sarah, being one hundred and four years old, had decided she didn't have a whole lot of reason to keep her words the kind and generous sort.

After my visit, I thought about these two ladies. I wondered about their differences in age and attitude. Does eighty years old seem old to someone who's one hundred and four years old?

What exactly is old?

I was recently asked to write about my age. The question was, is my age a number I try to hide or ignore? I think about my age and aging, but I don't wish to dwell upon it. However, I was never one to run from a challenge, so I gave this one a second thought after rolling my eyes and thinking my first thought: "Who comes up with these challenges that I don't want to think about, write about, or face?"

Am I old? If so, what does that mean?

I know I can't be twenty forever. And that's okay; when you're young, you're at the bottom of the life chain with nowhere to go but up. I have reached the age that I am today (which is younger than tomorrow) and am as healthy—maybe healthier—than I was thirty years ago. I am just as active and full of life and love—more, because I value both more.

I think back to the year I turned fifty. I was ranting to my father, "Papa! I am a half century old!"

He put his book down, slowly looked up at me, and calmly replied, "Try on three quarters of a century for a week or two…then call me." Age is a relative thing.

I don't want to admit my age on the chance that someone will judge me as less valuable because I have lived more years. There are too many negative assumptions associated with aging.

Then again, who says those assumptions are true? My mom never said they are. That could be the reason she still runs her own very busy business at the age of eighty-two. And look at all the Harley dudes. The majority of them have white hair. They seem to be sitting comfortably with their age.

I don't know what old is. I am old to those much younger, and I am young to those much older.

My age is not a number on a ruler that measures my abilities, nor does it rule my choices, and it doesn't line up with how I feel or think or act. It doesn't hold me back. If anything, it gives me freedom—freedom because with age comes experience, education, and maturity, and those things bring liberty.

I will get old or die trying. Perhaps if I recognize old age when I reach it, I'll write to you about it.

# Trying to Touch the Sky

I can't resist a swing set. Every time I see one on the side of the road during my summer travels, I stop and go. By the time summer is in full swing, so am I.

Winter here in the Maine mountains is beautiful for sure, but summer means freedom from bundles of clothing, cold, and snow. And freedom, once tasted, is difficult to refuse ever after.

A motionless swing is waste of an invitation to freedom and a revisitation of the lighthearted, untroubled days of childhood. A playground swing is a simple pendulum where time stops. Swinging on a swing set reminds you what it feels like to be a child, free from the disquiet of the adult world. Worries, woes, and responsibilities can't catch you when you're flying. Those things must tap their toes and wait—for yours are pointing toward heaven.

That first powerful push-off starts the journey. You take three giant steps backward, backing up as far as you can, preparing to let go, another step backward, and you're almost ready to soar. You're on your tiptoes, and then you lift your feet, and suddenly you aren't grounded to the world anymore. You are airborne, eight years old and carefree. You have backed up all the way to those sunny days of your youth. Your mind becomes as clear as the blue sky above you. This is the closest you—a mere mortal—will ever get to true flight. When you are swinging, you can touch the sky.

I believe that children have a sense that we were meant to have wings (even if those wings are solely in the mind or in the soul). That's why the swing set has been such a popular playground toy. (Didn't you hate it when all the swings were taken by the kids in your class who were faster than you?)

I no longer need a push, and I am well beyond the teen years of sitting on a swing, moving in a noncommitted manner usually from side to side, and kicking at that rock or that pebble under my foot. The years of pushing my children are bygone as well. Now it's my airtime. You should try it. It would make my heart giggle to drive down the road and see every swing on every playground occupied by an adult swinging and laughing, exercising the soul with wild abandon.

# A Moment in a Day Without End

IT WAS ONE OF THOSE DAYS THAT WOULDN'T DIE. IT WAS A STUBBORN, never-ending day that refused to show mercy, give up, and just end. Instead, it seemed to grow hotter and heavier and longer—longer than the line of cars at the bank drive-through window, longer than the lines at the stores, shops, and businesses where I needed to be in order to shorten my to-do list. The lines made the day (and the lines on the faces in those lines) longer.

The entire day seemed as if humanity was devoid of even one happy, satisfied soul. It was as if everyone was wearied by the worries of the world. It was a day of trudging. I wanted nothing more to do with it; I wanted to finish my errands and get home where I could be happy (or at least hide).

My last stop was the grocery store. My shopping was finished and so was I—almost, for I was once again in a long line at the check-out. Finally done, I was putting my change in my wallet and was about to leave when I heard the song on the store's intercom radio. It was a good song. I looked at the cashier. She tilted her head back and jutted her chin out as if to ask, "Can I help you with something else?"

I didn't want to leave just yet; I wanted to listen to the song, so I stalled. "This is a good song," I said to her.

Her eyes went brow-ward like she needed to see the song in the air to hear it. "You are right; this is a good song," she agreed, and her chin started doing the slightest of juts outward in tune to the music.

I began the slightest of head bangs. "I really like this song," I said.

The bag lady who had been listening to us began listening to it and then started a rhythmic ear-to-shoulder action. "I've always liked this song," she said.

We listened. We did our little moves. And then, the bag lady smiled.

And then, the cashier smiled.

And then, I smiled.

And then, the bad day was brighter, better. All because of a good song and strange moves shared with strangers.

I smiled all the way home and all the next day too, remembering that musical, magical moment in a day without end.

# Deer Aunt Dot

MY GRANDMOTHER LIVED TO BE NINETY-FIVE YEARS OLD. MY GREAT-grandmother lived to be one hundred and one. I have a great-aunt who is one hundred and four. (There is no sense putting my mother on this list—at a mere eighty-two years old, she's still too young to count.) The women in my family live for a long, long time. However, we do eventually die. Case in point: Great-aunt Dot died at the young age of eighty-eight. (If she hadn't died by accidental medication overdose, I'm sure she would have lived another fifteen years.) My then six-year-old daughter Emily attended Aunt Dot's funeral with me.

As a member of a Maine family with a heritage of hunting for sustenance, Emily had been acquainted with death since birth. But being from a family whose members live longer than most folks normally do, the death with which she was familiar was that of the animal kingdom, not the human sort. Great-aunt Dot's funeral was her first encounter with human mortality, and with an open casket at this one, Emily received a full education.

On the ride home Emily was uncharacteristically quiet. I asked her if everything was all right. She answered my question with one of her own. She wanted to know if Aunt Dot was dead. I told her yes; Aunt Dot had indeed passed away, and then I prepared myself to answer all her questions with compassion and explain the reality of death being part of life in a way that would not frighten her.

Emily had one question: "If Aunt Dot is dead, then why didn't she look like this?" She closed her eyes, tilted her head to her shoulder, and hung her tongue out the side of her mouth. She looked every bit like a dead deer.

After I stopped choking on my repressed laughter, I explained that as dear as Aunt Dot was to us, she was not a deer.

# All the World's a Stage

THE SCENE I WITNESSED ALL THOSE WEEKS AGO WAS LIKE THE FLASH OF A camera—gone in an instant, but a snapshot of it remains in my mind. It was of a large, burly construction worker who was watching a woman—a frilly blonde body of fluff. She was trying to stuff her tiny Hollywood dog into an oversized purse. The dog wasn't having any of it. There was no way it was going inside that purse, and the pup flailed his legs and paws in an attempt to be sans bag. The woman's quest was hindered by the encumbrances of her gender: jewelry and scarves, high heels, long nails, and a mass of purposely wildly coiffed curls.

The scene was comical; the most enjoyable part for me was watching him watch her. I could read his mind. "What is that woman doing?" Although he could see what she was doing—she was stuffing a dog into a purse. What he really wanted to know was, "Why is that woman stuffing a dog into a bag?"

I want to know what would possess a woman to carry a dog around in a purse. Aren't the burdens of the day heavy enough? I suppose it's easier to carry your burdens than drag them along behind you.

That scene was a moment of humanity I feel fortunate to have witnessed. It was like taking a break during a busy day and watching a theatrical comedy production. I enjoyed it immensely.

This next one certainly wasn't a comedy.

There was a young woman sitting under a large tree by the side of the road. I watched her stand up, her phone in hand. She pulled her arm back behind her shoulder as far as she could and, with a throw powered by fury, hurled her cell phone at the tree. When it hit the solid trunk it shattered into pieces. (I imagined her heart was doing the same.) I thought, "You poor thing." (Isn't it sad that people hurt people?) Then I thought, "Geez, girl, he might be a heartbreaker, but come on, honey—that was your phone! Now how are you going to call all your girlfriends?"

I was watching a soap opera, right there on Route 142. The thought that paying for cable service was a waste crossed my mind. Who needs reality TV when you can watch real live folks?

Not all the scenes that impress me involve people.

I was stuck in construction traffic at a place where the road had been destroyed by a disaster. As I waited, I looked around. Down over a steep embankment a balloon was entangled in the branches of a bush. It was a bright blue balloon with brilliant yellow letters announcing "Happy Birthday"—a colorful bit of happy in such a destroyed, black-and-white place, like a clown dancing and laughing at a funeral. I felt as though I were in the middle of a piece of fine expressionism, not unlike what I've seen at the Museum of Modern Art, and the emotions evoked were the same.

"All the world's a stage…" Well put, Mr. Shakespeare.

# The Accordion Lesson

THERE WERE TWO REASONS I TOOK MUSIC LESSONS AS A CHILD: MY mother's belief that playing an instrument makes you well-rounded, and the fact that I had a family heirloom instrument at my fingertips: her accordion. So I took lessons…and I struggled.

I struggled with every song, every note, and with getting my fingers on the correct keys and buttons every time. I persevered because having the opportunity to play my mother's beloved accordion—the one her father had gifted her—gave me a sense of pride and honor. It made me feel special. Besides, I would get better, right? After all, I love music and appreciate it. I love the emotions it evokes; I love its energy. It can lift me up and calm me down. I wanted to make music, so I practiced faithfully, despite a few challenges—like my size. I did not have the arm length necessary to expand the accordion's bellows. Consequently, the noise the instrument made could only be called music in the wildest of imaginations. It was choppy and often interrupted by my fidgeting as I tried to readjust the weighty bulk in my arms to squeeze the thing—which was almost bigger than me—closed. Still, I persevered and practiced for more than a year.

And then came that fateful day. My granny came to visit and brought with her a little girl and her granny. It came up in conversation that the other little girl played the accordion. The grannies were thrilled that their girls played the same instrument.

One clapped her hands together and exclaimed, "Isn't it wonderful?"

"Oh, yes! It's lovely!" said the other.

"Play for us!" they insisted.

I, being just a bit older, played first.

I labored. Each movement, every finger motion, every note was hard-won, and the tune carried jagged edges to prove it. The grannies listened patiently. When I finished, instead of patting her hands together in applause, my granny patted my arm and encouraged,

"That was nice, dear. Keep practicing, just keep practicing."

And then it was the other girl's turn. Her fingers danced on the ivory keys and black buttons, and the bellows opened and closed like the wings of an angel gliding across heaven; her music was the voice of that angel.

It was wonderful.

It was lovely.

And when she finished there was silence—a fascinated, appreciative silence like the silence of a theatre audience just seconds before a rousing standing ovation.

"How long have you been playing?" she was asked.

"Six months," she answered.

My granny said to her granny, "She's a natural."

There is a peace that enters your soul when you know that you know when something has ended. When the torment of wondering if you should continue has finally been put to rest and you don't need to wonder anymore.

Some people are meant to make beautiful music, while some people are meant to simply listen and appreciate.

I never touched the accordion again.

## *All in One*

A BUSY WORKING MOTHER OF FOUR EQUALLY BUSY YOUNG CHILDREN complained about her family's crazy summer days, "It seems we rush to do this so we can rush to do that! We are doing too many things, going in too many directions—so much so it seems we don't enjoy any of it!" Each fall she secretly feels relieved that all the fun days are over. That's so sad, but often, so very true.

I'm just as guilty. I was having one of those insanely busy days when I took a moment to think to myself, you know, you really should take a moment to get dressed. I grabbed two socks—not a pair, mind you—just two random socks from a laundry basket full of clothes (which will eventually be put in the washer again before they are put into a drawer). I looked at the mismatched pair and hesitated for a split second, waiting for that warning thought to bubble up from my subconscious and childhood, but when it did not I shrugged and thought, my eye colors don't match each other, why should my socks?

I was rushing to get dressed so I could rush to write the day's to-do list (I treat my days like I treat the dishwasher: cram one more thing in) so I could rush to do my gardening (a pastime I normally savor) so I could hurry up and pack for a highly anticipated trip to the coast. Then a little boy who was walking by stopped to tell me something, and in doing so, he stopped all my too-busy ways.

He's five now. He told me he's really five plus five because he had two birthday parties two days apart. As he explained, he held both his hands up, fingers spread wide because he was doubly excited. And as he stood before me, telling me about his parties and his gifts and his cake, the thrill of this one event shining through his eyes, I noticed his toes. They were curled down over the top of his flip-flops, not because his shoes are too small, but because his feet were shoved into them as far as they could go. His toes were hanging ten—like him, hanging onto and enjoying one thing: his birthday. From his fingers to his toes he was all in as far as he could go, but only for this

159

one celebration on this one single day. And because I was into too many things all at once and always thinking of the next thing to come before the first thing is done, I nearly missed the tiniest of pleasures and insight: the funny little toes of a young boy, all in and enjoying every single second of one single thing.

# Be Yourself

"BE YOURSELF" IS ONE OF MY MOTHER'S FAVORITE TIDBITS OF WISDOM, and she uses it often. Whenever I voiced concern over an upcoming event in my young life, she would say, "Just be yourself; you'll be fine." It seemed to me at the time she was pooh-poohing my anxiety, but as it turns out, she was right: I was me and everything was just fine. (On those occasions that being me was the worst thing to be, I at least survived.)

Be yourself. That's a courageous calling because being you is one of the scariest things to be (although, even after a lifetime of pondering, I can't figure out why we think this). We are reluctant to be who we are because we are afraid of what people will think of us. In truth, people are probably so busy worrying about themselves and what other people think of them, they aren't giving us a second thought. But we don't know that, so we get nervous and we let it affect us to the point that we are no longer us.

Recently, at my job as a ski coach to young kids, I told the driver of the Moose Caboose (a sled pulled behind a snowmobile that carries children and coaches up the slope) to "Give it the popcorn!"

Upon hearing that, another coach turned to me, and with a quizzical look on her face said, "I don't get you…not even one little bit."

I didn't have time to explain since the Moose Caboose driver obviously understood, and we were immediately pulled into motion up the hill.

It's a fact of life: some people just aren't going to understand you.

One of Maine's early citizens, Mabel Littlefield, was also an odd duck in mannerism and appearance. It was said her face could stop a clock. She had an extravagant love of jewelry and bedecked herself in glittering ornaments with wild abandon. She wore her favorite jewels constantly—no matter the situation or circumstance.

Her blunt neighbors said things to her such as, "It don't matter how much you pile on, Mabel. There won't never be nobody so dazzled by them chains that he'll be willing to git married to what's underneath." (As a fellow lover of diamonds and pearls, I can attest to the fact that's not what it's about!)

Mabel didn't let the opinions of others define her. She stayed true to herself, remaining friendly and pleasant…and jewel-bedecked. She piled on more, learned to captain her father's sloop, and for several years sailed lumber and fish between the Wells and Boston markets, becoming a successful, highly respected businesswoman. The only thing swaying on this determined woman were her necklaces as she stood firm in her deep, locked-down view of herself, directing her ship and her life—the wind in her hair, her dangling earrings tossing about like her ship on the waves.

I don't know if inwardly she cried, or if the taunts strengthened her resolve, or both, but I imagine she said to herself, "I don't care if I am ever loved. I am the captain of my own ship, and I stand at my helm, doing and wearing the things that I adore."

Her intelligence and demeanor eventually won her the prize catch: the most handsome, sought-after man in the area. They married (she at the ripe old age of twenty-eight!) and lived happily ever after. Remember, just be you.

# A Beautiful Thing

A GOOD NIGHT'S SLEEP IS A BEAUTIFUL THING.

I usually fall asleep to the sound of cows lowing. It's a forlorn sound, a lovely haunting song in the night. These cows are my friends; they live just up the road on another friend's farm. They provide the milk I drink, and I am always careful to thank them personally when I stroll past their pasture on my way to get a gallon of their raw offering. I often comment on their beautiful eyes. I'm sure they hear that a lot, but I remind them just the same because it doesn't cost a thing to be kind, even to a cow.

Occasionally, an owl from somewhere deep in the vast wooded wilderness that is my backyard serenades me to sleep. Who, who, who are you calling to, owl? You sound lonely. Are you crying for a lost love? Keep calling; perhaps your love will hear the tear in your voice and return.

Many nights I am soothed to sleep by bugs. I am amazed that those creepy, crawling things I run from during the day become God's orchestra at night. I'm not an expert on which insects are out there, or which makes what sound, but the song of the insects after dark is a perfectly harmonized, beautiful lullaby.

Last night was a different story—the usual animal noises were accompanied by a dog barking, and he barked—no, he yapped—continually for hours. I finally got up and shut my bedroom window. (I hate shutting my bedroom window!)

The noise penetrated the glass.

I got out of bed again, turned on the fan for white noise, and slunk back under the covers. The fan clicked. Click, click, click, click, click, click, click, click, click, click. (Continual clicks—so annoying, right?)

I got out of bed, turned off the fan, kicked it, then went downstairs to dig through my cosmetic bag in search of the earplugs I keep on hand for traveling. I found one. I shrugged at the lone plug, put

it in my ear, and went back to bed, smushing the world's largest ear-
plug, my pillow, against the earplug-less side of my head. I started to
doze off, then, in an almost able-to-dream state, I rolled to my other
side. The barking brought me back to full consciousness. I threw the
stupid, worthless pillow on the floor.

There comes a time in a night like this that the battle stops being
about the noise and starts being about devising ways to sleep through
it. You could work all night trying to come up with ways to mask the
disturbance, only to be more frustrated by your failed solutions than
the reason you need them. Sometimes, it's better to just give in. I realized this, growled, then gave in and got up for the day even though it
was only three o'clock in the morning. Yes, a good night's sleep is a
beautiful thing, but sometimes it's just too much work.

# I'm in the Dirt

I NEED HELP. I AM A MAINE GARDENER. I DON'T MEAN I NEED HELP because I attempt to grow fruit and vegetables in Maine—in the mountains, no less—for that's a sickness with no cure. What I mean is I need help because my garden is growing. I don't mean the vegetables are growing, although they are, I mean my gardens are growing in size and number...alarmingly so. And since it's my hand that plants, I have no one to blame but myself.

Maybe it's because so many of my friends are farmers and gardeners and I've grown a fondness for that horti-culture. Maybe I'm awed by the everyday miracle that a seed will feed. (I recently read that one dollar worth of seeds produces twenty dollars' worth of food.)

Maybe the size of my garden reflects my huge fascination with food facts. Did you know pumpkin seeds help you stay asleep? (I've always wanted a pumpkin patch, and soon mine will rival Charlie Brown's.) Did you know pumpkin is a fruit? Did you know bananas are not? They are an herb. Did you know rhubarb strengthens tooth enamel?

Maybe I'm just nuts. (Can we grow those here? If you know how, call me.)

I've planted an entire alphabet of squash—from acorn to zucchini—and when I look at my backyard, I see a sea of veggies: corn, carrots, cucumbers, and cabbage.

The plot thickens...

I'm in love with my compost pile—it's tall, dark, and rich. I pay more attention to what I feed it than what I fed my children. (I know they didn't get as many fruits and vegetables.) I remember asking my then-teenage daughter if she'd eaten a vegetable that particular day. After thinking for a moment she asked, "Does pepperoni count?"

I went out to lunch with a friend who had been out of the country pretty much our entire planting season. Laura wanted to know what I'd been doing while she was away.

"I've been gardening," I told her. "I put in a huge vegetable garden—two, actually. I've become obsessed; it's getting scary. I can't bring myself to throw out a seedling! I just build another garden for it! Someone has to stop me! Laura, please stop me!"

"Would you like some tomato plants?" she asked.

After a very brief, shocked silence, I blurted, "Of course!"

"How about some potatoes and onions?"

"YES! I don't have potatoes or onions! I need potatoes and onions!" I cried.

"Of course you do, because onions are fun to grow. I also have sunflower, nasturtiums, cosmos, and zinnia seeds, if you'd like."

I hung my head in shame and whimpered, "I want them all."

"Okay," Laura said. "I'll come up this afternoon and help you put them in your garden. I'll bring some romaine lettuce plants, too."

Now that's a good friend: if she can't lead a successful intervention, she will at least lend a hand with the addiction.

I need to get a grip—and I don't mean on the planting trowel—I mean on my passion for planting. I promise I will…tomorrow… today I need to put in three new tomato plants and a chocolate mint.

# Life Lines

SUFFERING IS THE ONE THING ALL PEOPLE EVERYWHERE EXPERIENCE. IT comes to each of us regardless of our station in life, our color, our religion, our location, how much or how little money we have, and even in spite of our outlook on life. Few other things are as universal— not happiness, as I am convinced there are those who never feel that, and not blessings, for I know a few who wouldn't recognize one if it slapped them upside their head. Troubles, tests, and trials are universal.

A friend of mine was recently in despair over a hurtful situation. "I'm counting my blessings so my troubles won't trouble me so much," she said. Wouldn't it be nice if our blessings negated our problems? Like hydrocortisone cream to a bug bite or ice to a burn? It simply does not work that way.

I read about a musician who had his first megahit song the same week that his son was born with a life-threatening medical condition. He tried to put this in perspective by saying, "Life's problems and pleasures are like railroad tracks; they run parallel to each other." It seems to me they are more like the center lines on the highway. The lines on your side of the road represent your blessings, your good times, your days of sunshine and laughter. The lines on the other side of the road are troubled days, days of worry, pain, and loss—the lines symbolize those days that put lines on your face.

There are times when the lines on both sides—the problems we encounter and the blessings we enjoy—are solid and run beside each other. There are times when the line on the other side is broken and on your side is solid. That represents short spurts of hurt running alongside days of solid peace. Perhaps the broken lines are on your side for a while—intermittent lines of blessings next to a line of grief. The lines never touch. They do not overlap, and they do not erase each other.

There are times when the solid yellow line is all yours, like a giant smile following you wherever you go. Those are the days of cruising along, enjoying the view, listening to your tunes, singing with the radio, loving life in your lane, and then BAM, it happens: a freshly painted, intense solid line on the other side of the road shows up.

Broken hearts, broken lives, broken life lines are inevitable. But there is one other thing exclusive to the human race: hope. We don't know what lies ahead; you can be sure there will be lines in your future, around the next bend, at the top of that hill in front of you, in the valley below. One solid line might be the brightest you'll ever see, and it could stretch for miles and miles without another line in sight—and with all those miles behind you, this line might be on your side of the road all the way ahead.

# The Diamond Miner

My home is a bed and breakfast, so there are strangers here all the time. I like that, because I enjoy meeting people—in fact, I love it. Everybody has a story, everybody is a story, and as a storyteller, other people's lives and experiences are my fodder, usually savored and digested over breakfast.

I like Will Roger's attitude when he said, "Strangers are just friends I haven't met yet." But there was this one time…

I came down the stairs to find a man in the hallway, looking over the guest book that lay open on the check-in table. Strange, for most arriving guests ring the doorbell. He saw me and proclaimed, "I'm meant to stay here."

One of the many things I've learned in my years as a B&B owner is to pay attention to those "red flags" that some folks wave. This guy had plenty of flags, and they were flying full-mast in a high wind.

He spoke again. "I was stood up at the altar yesterday, and when I saw that diamond," he pointed to the diamond logo painted on my Diamond Corner B&B business sign, "I knew I was supposed to live here."

Live here? Ummm…no.

I admit, I was unnerved. If this guy thought the diamond on my sign was his sign, imagine what I thought, with just my daughter and me living there alone!

Ever so calmly and as graciously as possible so as not to torch his flags, I maneuvered him out the door and onto the porch, while I tried to figure out what to do next.

"Well, I'm not actually taking guests right now," I lied.

"You can't turn me away!" He turned angry.

But still, there was something about him that seemed pathetic, desperate, and hurting. That was why, after excusing myself and telling him to sit and relax while I got us a cup of tea, I called the local clergyman, not the police. I explained the situation to the pastor and asked for advice and help. He said he'd be right over.

The pastor's forthright arrival surprised the intruder, who, because of this miscalculation, went away willingly with the minister.

Later that day, the pastor called me with his assessment. After spending the morning in deep conversation with the flag-waving man, he shooed him out of town. He explained, "As you have learned to recognize trouble people, I have likewise learned to recognize truly troubled people. This guy is not one of those; he is a con artist."

The diamond miner was a dirty gold digger.

Will this experience jerk me out of my Will Rogers mind-set on strangers?

Absolutely not.

# Old T's

THEY ARE OFTEN BENT OVER, AND MANY WALK WITH A LIMP. THEY HAVE gnarled hands, white hair, and countenances weathered from enduring many seasons.

How many of us see old folks and see just old people? I did, but then one day, I met an elderly gentleman who told me something about his past that made me look at the aged in a different light. This man sat beside me in the park, and during the course of our conversation, it came up that I grew up in the military. He was in the military well before I was born and went on to humbly tell me how he did the preflight maintenance on the B-29 *Enola Gay*. Of course, he had no idea the *Enola Gay* was going to drop an atomic bomb on Hiroshima, Japan. (Some say this act ended the war and sufferings of World War II.) He was just doing his job, he said. I was amazed to be sitting so close to that much history.

This encounter led me to remember another old man I met a long time ago in a nursing home. He had spent his life doing what he felt was right for his family, not what he felt was right for him. He explained he had always wanted a college education, but there was never any money for that. He had a family to support, so he spent his entire working life not as a doctor, lawyer, or businessman, but as a milkman for Grant's Dairy.

"I did it for them because I love them and because taking care of my family is what I was supposed to do," he told me.

"Do you have any regrets?" I asked.

He glanced at his bedside table cluttered with photos of loving family members and assured me, "Not even a moment's."

In the hustle and bustle of daily living, we often sideswipe people who have done amazing things in their lives. There's no help for that, of course; we can't know remarkable, out-of-the-ordinary things about others…unless someone invented a T-shirt to give us a clue. T-shirts stating, "I'm done, but this is what I did."

The *Enola Gay* mechanic's T-shirt would read, "I helped change the course of history."

The Grant's Dairy deliveryman's T-shirt would read "I gave up me for mine."

I know folks who would have the following on their shirts:

"I rescued the astronauts from a stormy sea after their reentry from space." (This man told me that the astronauts were so green with seasickness, they looked like aliens.)

"I lived in a one-room shanty with my husband and nine children in a tiny Eskimo village called Happy Valley."

(What would your T-shirt read?)

These T-shirts would have to have a special, magical quality so the words wouldn't appear to everyone or just anyone, therefore diluting them. The writing on the T-shirts would have to be invisible since people who do great things (even if it's a little great thing) don't boast, they just do them.

If you have a heart to care, if you truly wonder, truly appreciate and respect those who have lived a long life before you, the words on the shirt would be revealed to you.

How much technology would be involved in the creation of such a T-shirt? A gargantuan amount, I imagine—years' and years' worth, I would think. (Not necessarily in the T-shirts, but certainly in the ability to read them.) That would be a lot of work. Perhaps it would just be simpler to find the time to befriend our elderly neighbors.

# One of Those Days

I WAS IN THE CASHIER LINE AT WAL-MART, WAITING, OF COURSE, SINCE that's what we do in lines, when I noticed I was surrounded by beautiful people. These beauties smiled at me from the covers of the Hollywood magazines.

They are so perfect, aren't they?

And then there's us—not-so-perfect us.

There are certain things we expect out of life. Even those of us with the lowest of expectations expect our shoes to work. You put them on your feet in the morning and expect that they will be there when you take them off at night—that is, if you haven't taken them off yourself during the day.

I began that day with such confidence, but ended it at the end of the line in Wal-Mart with my shoes duct-taped to my feet. My shoes had decided that this would be the day they quit serving me. Both, just moments apart, came apart, and left a trail behind me of silver and gold plastic beads that had graced the straps. One by one, the beads fell from grace and left me, leaving me grocery shopping with broken shoes (not an easy feat).

I curled my toes around the Y-strap, but because the top of the sandal was no longer attached to the sides of the sole, the bottom of my shoe swung around and repeatedly slapped me in the ankle. I tried shuffling. Shuffle-shopping ought to be an Olympic sport— it's that challenging. I did the only thing I could do: I duct-taped my shoes to my feet (every Mainer has duct tape in their vehicle). I considered going barefoot, but the thought of being escorted out of Wal-Mart for violating its "no shoes, no service" policy was just too much humiliation to handle. Walking around with duct tape wrapped around my feet was enough disgrace for one day. I do have my limits.

So there I was in line, my feet sweating in duct tape with all of Hollywood perfection staring at me—people with gleaming teeth, sparkling eyes, and flawless hair. My hair, after enduring a day of errands in the sweltering heat, looked as if it was not professionally coiffed, but coughed up.

Days such as these keep me humble.

## Short and Sweet

RECENTLY I ASKED AN ACQUAINTANCE THE USUAL "HOW ARE YOU?" YOU know, that typical question you ask when you see someone you sort of know. The answer I received was far from usual and certainly not what I expected to hear.

She said, "I've been in and out of the hospital for weeks with this blasted brain tumor!"

My first thought was, did she just say what I think she said? Indeed she had, and she went on to say that the doctors finally have her headache under control.

Should I ask her about the tumor, or should I ignore it by saying something noncommittal like, "Oh, well, I'm glad you're feeling better," then move the conversation in another direction? Does she want to talk about it? Do I? Those questions raced through my mind. I put my fear of the unknown (the number one reason people don't talk about death) aside. Because life can be very heavy-duty, it's important to be brave; it's essential to put aside our fears for the sake of others who are facing theirs.

"You have a brain tumor?" I gave her the invitation to talk.

She didn't speak; she nodded.

"What is your prognosis?" I jumped in with both feet.

"I am going to die," she said matter-of-factly. Before I could register a reaction, she continued, "But my prognosis is good. Do you want to know why?"

It was my turn to nod.

She explained herself by talking about someone else. "My neighbor Martha was a perfectly healthy woman, busy and full of life, but last month she died suddenly and unexpectedly of a cerebral hemorrhage. Martha didn't have time to say good-bye to her husband, children, or grandchildren. She didn't have time to say one more 'I love you,' no time to call an old friend, no time to right wrongs, no time to realize how precious time is. My prognosis is good

175

because I have today and most likely tomorrow. I have time. I have more time than many others and for that, I am thankful," she said.

And I am thankful for the reminder to take the time while I have it to do those exact things and that life (like this story) is short… and sweet.

# The Battle for Independence

MY PHONE RANG.

"Hello?"

"Dorothy?" The voice on the other end of the line was weak and shaky.

"I'm sorry," I told the lady, "you have the wrong number."

She apologized and hung up. My phone rang again.

"Hello?"

"Dorothy?"

"Nope, still the wrong number." She apologized profusely and hung up. When she called the third time she was mortified and close to tears to learn she had once again misdialed. I lightened the moment by telling her I had been washing windows and welcomed the distraction.

"Who are you trying to call?" I asked her.

"My daughter, Dorothy," she answered.

"Where do you live?" I thought if she was nearby, I'd go dial the number for her, but she was calling from a faraway nursing home.

"I'm certain the nurse will dial your daughter's number for you," I suggested.

"I don't want her help," was her spirited reply. I heard a spark of trampled-upon independence in her voice. I wondered if being in a nursing home and needing help with so much, she wanted to do this one thing on her own.

"I'll ask the operator!" she said.

"Okay, good luck," I said, and we hung up.

My phone rang.

"Hello?"

"Dorothy?"

"You didn't ask the operator for help, did you?"

She sighed. We chatted for a while. "This isn't how I used to sound," she said. "I sound like this because I find it difficult to breathe now."

"Why?" I asked.

"Because I'm fat. I'm really very fat." Her honesty made me smile, although her situation made me say, "Oh, you poor thing! Well, maybe you will let the nurses help you with that."

"Did you get your windows cleaned?" she wanted to know.

"Yes, most of them, but the morning sun shines through and I can see all the spots I missed."

"How many windows do you have?"

"Thirty-nine," I said.

"Oh, my! Do you have a husband?"

"No, but I have a dog." She laughed—a big, big belly laugh.

She asked me my age; I told her.

I asked her age; she told me.

Too close for comfort.

It was obvious this woman kept all her troubles just inside her lips so every time her mouth opened, they'd spill out. Perhaps that's a good thing. Maybe that kept her troubles out of her heart, where they could cause real damage.

Out of the blue she said, "I had to give my car away."

"Wow!" I thought. "Slam!" Freedom gone—given away, yet stolen. I had no idea how to answer. Thankfully she didn't give me a chance to leave the sound of silence.

"But..." she continued, "my daughter Dorothy is going to move here and take me home. I want my own home."

"Of course you do!" I said. "Just don't get one with thirty-nine windows!"

Again she laughed.

"But it's a battle." She became serious once more.

"Yes, of course it is; all worthwhile things are," I supposed. "But you keep fighting, okay? Keep trying to call Dorothy. You'll get your independence back," I hoped. "And when you have won all your battles, call me," I said. "Call me from your own phone, from your own home."

"I will do that, dear, but…" She hesitated. "I don't have your number."

"Yes, Old Warrior," I said, "You do."

# The Facts of Life

HERE YOU GO, GRADUATES, OUT OF SCHOOL AND OUT ON YOUR OWN— into adulthood, into the world, into life. Do you know the facts of life?

One fact of life is this: you are an intelligent being. Read, study, learn—read everything, even drivel. Because you are an intelligent being, you have the ability to entertain the thoughts and ideas of another without embracing them as your own. How will you recognize the truth if you're not familiar with the lie? Be a watchman for that truth and then, having found it, live it. Stand firm in what you believe, even if you are standing alone. The truth will win in the end and everyone will know it; that's the beauty of it.

Another fact of life is this: life is challenging; it's tough and often cruel. Don't let it harden you, don't lose who you are. Losing yourself can happen slowly—miniscule pieces of you can fall away a little at a time so that it is almost indiscernible. Unlike losing your car keys, you won't notice right away until one day you look in the mirror and a stranger is looking back at you. Don't let the world do that to you. Take time to collect yourself by reflecting on your purpose in life (yes, you have a purpose—or two, or three…). May that time of reflection keep your reflection pure.

Another fact of life is that true contentment can be lost in the pursuit of prosperity. There is nothing wrong with mastering the talent of making money; it's when you make money your master that your life becomes unbalanced. Money is a tool to run the machine, but it is not the driver. Don't be deceived. Just because money can buy you the best hiking boots doesn't mean it will put you on the right path.

A fact of life: the world is selfish. Selfishness hurts. But the world can't hurt you if you don't want anything from it. Focus your desires on things not of this world: being kind, being better, and helping others to help themselves when and where you can. Rise above the ugliness, but always be that rare and beautiful thing willing to stoop down to help another up—even if you have to use both hands.

A fact of life is this: a lot of people incorrectly define love. Love isn't about changing a person or people to suit your emotional needs. Love is the opposite. It's about constraining yourself from attempting to transform another. Love doesn't have a list of requirements behind it—the word is short and easy to pronounce for a reason. It's meant to be that way because it is enough. Love is enough. It's about loving people the way they are, with their faults and failures, not in spite of them. True love is powerful enough on its own to change those things that need changing. And if that change doesn't come, maybe the other person isn't the one in need of it.

Now, off you go; it's up to you, and all the choices are now yours to make. And that is the truest fact of life.

# The Story of the Milkweed Seed

THE DAY WAS COLD AND WINDY, BUT THE SUN WAS SHINING IN THE FRIGID berry-blue Jell-O sky—a day like so many mid-fall days here in western Maine. I was sitting in my fold-up travel chair, contently listening to my girlfriends talk about quilts and fiddlers and an incident when a different gaggle of women broke out in the song "Goodnight Irene."

As my friends chatted, I tipped my head back to watch a cloud float along (as clouds are want to do) when a lone milkweed seed gliding above the treetops caught my eye. She was beautiful, dainty, and delicate; she looked like the tiniest ballerina pirouetting across a heavenly stage. An insignificant seed, yes, but her twirls and swirls, dips and risings made her journey seem a ballet.

She narrowly escaped entrapment in the branches of a leafless tree—the smaller offshoot branches looked very much like the thorns of a rosebush. I rooted for her, then breathed a sigh of relief when she exited the other side and disappeared with the wind.

I wanted to know more about this plant, so upon returning home, I found my book on flowers and read about the milkweed. It's common, it's intrusive, it's poisonous, and it's sort of ugly. None of these attributes are highly prized by gardeners. I felt sorry for it. I also discovered the one and only usefulness of a milkweed is to feed insects. I put my plant book down and thought about that, more than mildly disappointed. This lovely, dancing, twirling seed seemed more destined to be a flower of pure heavenly scent, one that perfumers spend thousands of days and dollars to recreate, or at least she should be a plant coveted for her miraculous medicinal properties. But no, she is simply meant to feed bugs and larvae. It is her life's purpose, the reason she exists. It's in her DNA and she knows it (but does she know how far down on the ladder of success her rung is?). She is not destined for fame—still, she does what she does in a lovely celebration of dance, and her lowly journey is full of grace and beauty.

I picked up my book again and continued to read about this

odd plant and its mismatched, magnificent seed. That is when I read the sentence that made me smile and understand and fall in love: there is a larva that is dependent solely on her for sustenance and growth—the larva of the monarch butterfly. The monarch, that wonderfully beautiful creature, cannot come into being without the common milkweed.

# This Girl's Life

ONCE UPON A TIME THERE WAS A LITTLE GIRL. THIS LITTLE GIRL WAS sort of a dork, and she did weird things like walk around her neighborhood singing hymns she'd learned in Sunday school. She wasn't singing while she played, or singing while she walked to a particular destination, she was just singing and walking to simply walk and sing because that's what she loved to do—oblivious to anyone who might be listening.

This little girl was lost in the lineup of a big, boisterous family, but she didn't suffer because of it, for she never noticed that she wasn't noticed. She lived in her own little world—not a world of make-believe, but a world of believing she would be given her heart's desire, simply because it was pure. She pretended the world was full of fairies, princesses, and goodness. She wanted to build an orphanage to give children a safe home.

She wanted to have a little girl of her own and name her Beauty (because all little girls are beauty). She loved flowers, collected pretty rocks, and sought precious things like fireflies and pinecones.

She loved to dance.

She tried to keep up with her big brother and his friends. She wore boys' pants, peed standing up, and read their thought-provoking books like *The Hobbit*, but couldn't get past the fascination that the characters lived in hobbit houses.

She was a little bit of a rebel.

Her hair was always a mess of wayward, tangled strands and she giggled...a lot. She was a terrible student, but only because she couldn't be bothered to be a good one.

This little girl matured to adulthood.

Now she is a terrible student because she simply can't be bothered to learn stuff other people think she should learn. She studies people instead...and laughs a lot.

Her hair is graying; it's a worse mess than ever. She is a rebel who has mellowed because aging, raging hearts soften. She keeps up with the big boys on skis, four-wheelers, snowmobiles, and Jeeps, but has grown secure enough to sit down to pee. She reads thought-provoking books (and understands some of them), but also reads books on how to build hobbit and fairy houses.

She dances every chance she gets.

She tends the flowers she loves, collects rocks, and pursues precious things like friendship and peace (and pinecones).

She has three beautiful girls of her own. She lives in her own little corner of the world and opens her home to children who need a safe place to stay. She pretends the world is a beautiful place (every once in a while it shows her that yes, indeed, it can be). She isn't noticed much, but doesn't suffer from that because she has been noticed by someone who calls her Beauty. She still sings, although with a different voice—it is now a voice of written words. She writes just for the joy of it (sometimes dorky stuff), but her words are her song, even if no one is listening.

She's happy because she's proof that little girls' lives don't have to be lived once upon a time.

# Tuesday, February 12th

THE CREAMER IN MY MORNING COFFEE CURDLED AND LOOKED LIKE SMALL boats swirling around in a muddy sea. That was the first clue. I should have paid heed and gone back to bed and hidden there, but being forever hopeful, I forged on with my day: a few chores, a couple errands, and a dental appointment, then onto work. Just another day.

My first task was to process my pumpkin for baked goods—the same pumpkin I had carefully tended and lovingly nurtured all summer. After laboriously harvesting it last fall, I carefully placed it in the perfect spot to cure. When I went to gather it I discovered it had rotted—black decay straight through.

So, I sat down and wrote my weekly newspaper column on Maine rural life, then, meaning to delete one sentence, I accidentally deleted all four hundred words! When the shock of my destruction wore off, I noticed it was time for my dental appointment. I consoled myself, "At least I'm not ruining a *good* day by going to the dentist."

The gas pump froze and refused to give me more than five dollars and sixteen cents worth of fuel. I had to go inside to pay in order to get enough gas to get me where I needed to go, which was to the market, where the line was long with male customers (snowmobilers, to be exact), and they couldn't seem to find the peanut butter or the door to leave. They made me late for the dentist.

The dentist took me in anyway and stabbed my tender gums with sharp needles, prodded them with horror-movie props, and scraped my sensitive teeth. When the torture was finished, the hygienist said, "All done. We don't need to see you again for a while."

"I'll miss you desperately," I said through numbed mouth.

When I opened my checkbook to pay, I discovered it was empty. No checks. No big deal really, but also no big discount for paying at the time of service.

On the way home a log truck in front of me sprayed my windshield with a brown covering. (It was very nearly the color of my ruined morning coffee, as if I needed a reminder of the day's start.) I pushed the windshield-washer button, and the blades smeared the mocha mess across the glass. The tank for windshield washer fluid was empty, just like my checkbook. I would have had an inkling that it needed filling, but the warning light had been on for so long that the bulb had burnt out, and I, lacking that reminder, had forgotten. (I wish that annoying "check engine" light bulb would also have the manners to stop glaring at me and burn out, too.)

I next went to work where I teach small children to ski. I was assigned a three-year-old crier who had decided to make it her life's ambition to never, ever ski no matter what, and she was quite vocal on the matter. Plus, she had a runny nose. Did I have tissues? Of course not; they must have been with my checks and my windshield washer fluid.

Finally, at day's end, I was able to go home—to rest and peace I had hoped, but no—my dog Harry had somehow weaseled out of his collar and run off. A man drove into my driveway to tell me Harry was in the road. Yup, there he was, pooping in the middle of Route 27 with a line of cars from both directions forced to stop to watch his show.

Come what may the rest of this day (which is one to remember and one to try to forget), I'll remain ever hopeful.

After all, it's only one day, and I have a brand new container of cream for tomorrow's coffee.

## *Words From the Heart*

---

IT HAS BEEN WRITTEN: THE WORDS YOU SPEAK COME FROM YOUR HEART. Often, these words are hints about who we truly are, how we are feeling, or what we are experiencing that particular day. Our world swirls around us, funnels into our souls, and drips out of our mouths in revealing words—whether we realize it or not.

How to tell when your daughter is distracted:

"Emily, what's the name of the song your sister Holland was playing on her guitar Easter Sunday? I can't remember the musician's name, so I can't look it up on the Internet."

Emily replied, "I don't know, Mom, but if you know the musician's name, you can look it up on the Internet."

How to realize your girlfriend is exhausted:

"This is such a big, huge world with so many things in it!" appreciated girlfriend number one.

"Aren't you glad we don't have to clean it?" sighed girlfriend number two.

How to tell that your friend is proud to be a humble Mainer:

As we were riding up the chairlift at Sugarloaf, the local ski resort, a skier from away was telling us how he was looking for the perfect vacation home in our area. His second home had to meet certain specifications: it had to be in the perfect location, it had to be built of specific materials, it had to have this, it had to have that, and so on.

My friend Cathy piped up and proudly announced, "We brought our camp over from Cutler on the back of a dump truck."

The out-of-towner stuttered for a bit, and then asked, "Do you mean it was a beach house?"

"Oh, no, no," Cathy explained, "It was an old clam shack."

How to know that a friend is nipping her involvement in your hobby in the bud:

"Have you ever sewn a smelt to a fish line?"

"No, and your next question should be, 'Do you ever want to?'"

How to be reminded that your friend is a fisherman:

While at the University of Maine at Farmington's orchestra concert, my friend looked up from the concert program's list of musicians and their instruments and asked me, "Which one is the bass?"

When I stopped snorting (because it would have been improper to laugh out loud), I told her, "It's pronounced *base.*"

How to learn that someone needs support and encouragement:

This past winter, while teaching a group of young people to ski, I watched as one young man observed his fellow (and more capable) classmates ski down the hill in front of him. With something akin to hopelessness written across his face, he reassured himself with a whispered, "This is not a team sport."

If you listen with your heart to your friends and family, you'll hear a lot more than just what they are saying.

# About Nothing

HER HOUSE WAS WALL-TO-WALL PEOPLE. EVERY ROOM WAS FULL OF laughing, conversing folks, some she knew and some she did not. Colleagues, clients, acquaintances, friends, family—they were all there, crowding her. She was surrounded. She could see her child on the other side of one room waving to her and her husband on the opposite side of another room, waiting for her. But her house was too full, and she could not get through the throng of folks. As she tried to push her way through the crowd, she frantically repeated, "I did not plan this party! I did not plan this party!"

After my friend recounted this dream to me, I told her it didn't take an interpreter to understand the meaning. "Your days are so full they are spilling over into your nights," I said. "And it seems you feel a little out of control."

She nodded her head in agreement, held up her finger and thumb (indicating a small amount), and with a not-so-small amount of sarcasm, mouthed the words, "Just a little."

"Some days it feels like I'm drowning," she complained.

Haven't we all had days—weeks—like that? Wouldn't it be nice to have a few days with no bodies? Haven't we all wished for a day when nobody called, nobody complained, nobody bothered us, nobody needed to eat? We dream of a day of no demands on our time, our checkbooks, or our emotions. Our party of choice would be a calm tea party for one. And having enjoyed that day so much, wouldn't we wish for a never-ending, nice, quiet, no-nonsense life?

I know of a woman who accomplished just that. This woman—nobody really knows why—didn't want the chaos and strife of life, so in an effort to shield herself from the mess that life often is, she isolated herself from the world. She chose not to have a family or pets or a home—not even a garden, because all those things cost. They cost time, money, peace of mind, and piece of heart. So she lived a quiet life devoid of property and payments, friends and family, stress, striving and strain. Most folks around town didn't even know she existed. Those who did know of her knew only one thing: that she lived alone in tiny rented apartment and she kept to herself, spending her days doing nothing, seeing nobody, living a calm life in a cocoon.

And then, in the prime of life, she died. The autopsy report would later reveal that she didn't die of coronary artery disease, cancer, kidney disease, infection, or stroke. She didn't even have a cold. She didn't have anything.

I think she died of nothing.

I am writing this from my raft (my desk). My home right now is a sea of chaos—family, friends, noise, and activity. (So please, forgive any grammatical errors!) I feel as if I'm drowning in it all, and that's okay because it might be a scarier, more exhausting way to go, but I'd rather drown in a sea of too much than die of thirst.

# The Good, The Bad, and The Ugly:
## Two Halloween Stories and One That Should Be

### The Good

I had an orange plastic jack-o'-lantern with a hole in the top. The boy standing next to me had a half-pint juice box container. We were both trick-or-treating, but he was for a cause: UNICEF, The United Nations Children's Emergency Fund. I don't remember his name or even if he was a friend, I only remember he was standing beside me as the lady with the candy came to the door. She filled the hole in my pumpkin's head and then gave the boy a nickel for his UNICEF juice box. She offered him a candy but he politely refused, saying, "No treats for me this year. I'm trick-or-treating for children in need."

She insisted, "Take a little something for yourself."

He declined, "Thank you, but no. And besides, I don't have a place to put candy."

The lady was adamant, determined to bless this little do-good-er. She placed a solitary piece of round, hard candy on the coin slot of his juice carton. The two of us watched as it rolled to the edge, shimmied there for a nanosecond, then rolled back the other way to do the same on the other edge. Back and forth, back and forth it went. We stared, mere innocent children caught in the battle of wills. (Will the candy fall so he wins, or will it stay on the juice box to give her the victory?) The candy slowed near the center; it jiggled; it wobbled; then, with one last shudder, it gave up and balanced. He looked at me. I looked at him. We awkwardly shrugged at each other.

The boy didn't put the candy in his pocket. I imagine he felt that if he did, the act of doing for himself would be a do-gooder's undoing. Instead, in order to keep the piece from falling where it may, this little boy walked away, balancing his juice box container just so. That way the woman's goodie would stay put, outside his pocket, yet inside her kindness, keeping his goodness balanced.

## The Bad

The neighborhood bad boy thought it would be a good idea to help himself to the entire basket of Halloween candy that the nice lady left unattended on her front stoop, so that's exactly what he did: he stole it all. He dumped the basket into his candy bag, snickering like the evil ghost he was.

A thief's second impulse is always to run, and that's exactly what he did next: he turned and ran. In his frenzied escape, he tripped on the hem of his ghost sheet and fell, and the contents of his bag spilled out and flew helter-skelter across the yard. The other trick-or-treaters were on the spilled contents like a flock of cedar waxwings on a ripe highbush cranberry. They took every candy bar, every gumdrop, every Tootsie Roll.

My mind's eye can still see him: a white ghost crawling around on green grass and all fours, yelling and screaming and clawing to retrieve the pieces of his stolen spilled candy. But every stolen piece was stolen.

## The Ugly

Because my father's military career took us to a new home in Charleston, South Carolina, I was the new girl in school, about to have a new, exclusively southern experience.

My first day in class found me desperately trying to turn my attention away from my tickling foot to what my seventh-grade teacher was saying through her thick southern accent. When I could ignore it no longer, I took my shoe off with the intention of scratching that itch, only to find the origin of it: a large-as-my-thumb, uglier-than-sin cockroach. It scurried out of my shoe and across the beige tiles of the classroom floor and disappeared into a crack in the baseboard.

I felt woozy. My eyes rolled toward the back of my head. I gagged and fought waves of nausea. Then (and not without a bit of effort to stay conscious) I raised my hand and with a weak, barely audible voice, asked to go home.

"Why?" the teacher wanted to know.

"There was a cockroach in my shoe."

Every eye in the class turned toward me. Southerners are ac-
customed to cockroaches, so nobody understood my repulsion. I myself cannot explain the psychology of the aversion. I lay it at the feet
(of which they have too many) of their ugliness and the fact that
something so ugly secretly hitched a ride in my footwear. I know cockroaches aren't poisonous, but they scurry. I know they don't bite, but
they crunch when you squish them underfoot. And besides, they are
ugly.

I was allowed to go home, but not to Maine. That made me
ugly. (Only a Mainer understands that.)

# A Happy? New Year

"Enjoy life more." That resolution tops the top-ten list of most popular New Year's resolutions. The next most popular are:

quit drinking

quit smoking

lose weight

exercise

get out of debt

get organized

It seems to me that if one accomplishes all those, the first resolution has been negated.

It has become our habit to start the new year in the negative. No wonder most resolutions fail!

The New Year's celebration has always been about change. It began in Babylonian times in the month of March. Eventually the Romans changed it to January in honor of their god Janus, the two-faced god who looked backward into the old year, yet also forward into the new. This is when the practice of making New Year's resolutions began. (The irony of making life changes to please something two-faced is not lost on me.) But still, the resolutions of that era had a moral flavor, mostly to be good to others. This leads me to understand another reason why so many of our resolves fail: we fail to change the direction of our habits because we've changed the direction of our focus. The Romans made resolutions for the betterment of others, but somewhere along the line, our focus turned internal; we make resolutions for us. (And since we aren't going to punish ourselves when we are unsuccessful, we easily fail.)

Instead of attempting to stop our old personal undesirable habits, we should take a lesson from history and focus on being good to others. (You can't fail when you resolve to be good to someone else.) This is exactly what the resolutions of the first resolutioners were. Medieval knights would recommit their practice of chivalry toward one another. The Puritans of New England resolved to "better employ their talents." (Who reaps the benefits of one's talent? Others do, of course.)

Those are resolutions I can live with.

So, this year, I resolve not to make New Year's resolutions, but rather I resolve not to bring last year's failures into this year's possibilities.

That should make for a very happy new year.

I think a few folks these days could learn a lot from doing the same.

PART SIX

*Ski School:
An Education*

# A Ride into a Child's Mind

I work at Sugarloaf Mountain Resort, teaching children to ski. The chairlift ride is a perfect opportunity to get to know the kids. The conversations we have are some of the most enjoyable I've ever experienced.

Children have a simple understanding of how things work. For this reason, I enjoy asking them unusual questions. I love the answers to which I am treated.

"Why do bunnies hop?" I asked a five-year-old boy.

"My dad doesn't know and so neither do I," he said, unconcerned that he didn't know.

"How do you know your dad doesn't know?" I asked.

"Because he would have told me," he explained.

Dad may not have told this child about bunnies hopping, but this child's answer told me oodles about this wonderful, involved dad.

"Why do bunnies hop?" I asked a six-year-old.

"I have no idea; I want to be a paleontologist," she said.

Thrown off guard, I was silenced and tried to remember what a paleontologist does. While I was thinking, she spelled it: "p-a-l-e-o-n-t-o-l-o-g-i-s-t."

"Why do bunnies hop?" I asked a seven-year-old boy.

"So they can jump out of the way of the animals that want to eat them," he said. (Here's proof that knowing it all can take the fun out of life.)

"Why do bunnies hop?" I asked a three-year-old. She looked at me, her brow furrowed. I could read her mind; she was wondering if this was a trick question.

"Don't you know?" she wanted to know.

I shook my head.

"Because…" She spread her hands out in front of her and explained the simple. "They're bunnies!"

And that was the answer I had been looking for.

We expect to get certain things out of life, and I believe we have trained our kids to think the same.

One little guy proudly showed me his wiggly front tooth.

"Be careful," I warned. "I know a little girl who did that. Her tooth fell out and landed in the snow…" I pointed to the ground several dozen feet below us, "…way down there, and it was lost forever!"

He looked at me with eyes as wide as half dollars. "*WHAT?*" He was horrified. "No money from the tooth fairy? What a rip-off!" he yelled.

Many times, I have no control over the topic.

I asked a four-year-old if she was having chicken fingers for lunch, because four-year-olds usually go for that sort of thing.

"I'm a vegetarian," she said.

"I guess that answers my question," I said.

"Are you a vegetarian?" she wanted to know.

"No, I'm not," I answered.

"So, you're a meat-eater," she stated matter-of-factly.

"Yes, I am," I said (although "meat-eater" isn't exactly what I see when I look in the mirror).

"Why are you?"

"Why am I a meat-eater?"

She nodded.

I pondered.

"Because I never was not one," I supposed.

She looked at me and frowned.

"Maybe it's because I'm from Maine."

She seemed to understand that better.

The next day as we settled in on the chairlift ride, the subject came up again.

"I told my mother you are a meat-eater," she blurted out.

"Did you tell her I ate a moose?" I blurted back.

Her jaw dropped (you could have put a moose in her mouth).

I treasure the conversations I have with these children; they never cease to amaze me. It only takes a few short minutes riding up the chairlift in my world to be enlightened by theirs.

# *No Kidding Around*

I LIKE WORKING WITH KIDS. THEY DON'T MINCE WORDS; THEY TELL IT like it is. This is one reason I choose to coach the three-to-six-year-old age group at ski school.

Kids let you know exactly where they stand. They are genuine, blunt, and often brutally honest. I would much rather deal with their straightforward ways than try to understand the hidden agendas so frequently found in the adult world.

If kids are involved in a conspiracy against you, they are candid about it. Here's an example.

No matter what I suggested we do in our ski lesson or where we go, four-year-old Luke shot it down.

"Let's go on the chairlift," I said.

"That's a bad idea," he countered.

"Okay, how about if we work on turning to stop?"

He shook his head. "That's a bad idea."

"Let's practice our turns, then," I suggested.

"That's a really bad idea."

I finally asked him why he always says, "That's a bad idea."

Without apology, he admitted, "Because my friend Matthew told me to." (I think having a talk with Matthew might be a good idea.)

Kids don't pretend to be anything except exactly who they are.

I coached a five-year-old chatterbox on a bitterly cold day as she jibber-jabbered about a thousand things, from chocolate chip cookies to chipmunks. I tried to pull her neck-up over her nose and cheeks to protect them from the cold, but she refused because doing so would cover her mouth and she complained, "I can't hear myself talk."

It doesn't occur to children to be limited by the improbabilities in life.

A little girl, when asked by her mother if she liked skiing, shivered and answered, "Yes, but I'd like it better in the summer."

With kids, what's important is what's important.

After many failed attempts, three-year-old Olivia finally succeeded at stopping herself while on skis, and when she did, I whooped and hollered, "Yeah, Olivia! Woot, woot! You did a GREAT job!"

She looked at me, pointed to her eyes, batted them, and asked, "Are my eyes pretty?"

When children require assistance, they don't need psychotherapy or self-help books to learn how to ask for it. They simply recognize they need help and without shame or self-condemnation, they speak up.

While dressing one child to go outside, I glanced up to see a three-year-old who had just come out of the little boys' room. He turned his bare behind to the room, pointed to his partially exposed buttocks, and called out, "Is this clean?"

One of my favorite things about children is their understanding of the value of aging. We adults are so against growing older, but children are keenly aware of the benefits of maturity.

"Mom said when I'm six, I can get ski poles," said one hopeful skier.

Oh, the wisdom of being excited about the advantages of advancing on the timeline of life, even when that advancement comes in small (often hard-won) increments.

"How old are you, Ben?" I asked.

"I'm four and a third," he bragged.

Children remind me that we don't need years of experience to know what matters most in life. Their wisdom at such a young age is proof that we are born with the seeds of fundamental truths in our hearts. I am grateful for these little things who are grateful for the little things, no matter where they are on the calendar of life.

## Climbing the Ladder

"What is the best part about being six?" I asked Gavin.

"I get to be in a grade," he answered.

"What is the best part about being three?" I asked Olivia.

"I'm three and a half," she indignantly informed me.

"Oh, excuse me!" I tried again, "What's the best part about being three and a half?"

She leaned toward me and lowered her voice (perhaps because speaking the words would make the blessing bubble burst) and whispered, "They let you ski."

"What is the best part about being five?" I asked Anna.

"You can swing."

"Why can't you swing when you're four?"

"You can, but it's really difficult," she said.

Four-year-old Addie had it all figured out. When I asked her the best part of being her age, she said, "It's all about getting bigger."

## Simple Pleasures

"What is the best part about being six years old?"

"I get to do the dishes," Mark said.

"Why do you like to do the dishes?" I asked him.

"Because I can see out the window and watch Hunter play."

"Who is Hunter?"

"My cat."

Jenna told me the best part about being five years old is she now hugs her mom.

"That is so sweet, Jenna," I told her. "I'm wondering, though, why you didn't hug your mom when you were four years old."

"Because that's when she hugged me."

## Small Victories in Big Battles

Nick turned five years old the day I asked him the question, "What are you going to be able to do now that you're five that you couldn't do when you were four?"

His answer was almost immediate; he'd obviously already given this some thought, this being the very day of change.

"I'm going to race on my Wii and not crash into something. I always crash into something," he confessed.

"We all crash into things, Nick," I told him. "But only sometimes," I quickly added.

"I know," he sighed. "I'm just going to try."

## Liberty and the Pursuit of Happiness

Five-and-a-half-year-old Nate was a deep thinker. When I asked him what was most important in his life, he told me, "Family." Then after a brief pause, he added, "And freedom."

"Freedom?" I wanted more.

"Yeah, it's not like it was back when people owned people," he explained.

"I see." I was amazed at this child's mature thinking. He then renewed my faith in childhood innocence when he added, "And my toys are important, too."

When I asked Liam what the best part of being his age was, he thought for a moment, then nonchalantly shrugged his shoulders and answered, "It's just a number."

Having the opportunity to view life through the eyes of a child is a blessing and the best part of me being my age.

# Kid Stuff

As you probably know, I teach young children to ski at the local resort, Sugarloaf. I typically end the season by sharing a few kid stories. Here are this season's:

"When are you and I skiing together?" I asked the little miss as I dressed her to go skiing with another coach.

"We better wait until your back is better," she answered.

I had never complained about my back, because there's no reason to. "My back? My back is fine," is what I said, but I was thinking, "What in the world is this child talking about?"

"You know, your spine."

"My spine?! My spine is perfectly healthy," I assured her.

And then she said, "This is an arabesque!" and she did a ballet arabesque with her ski boots on.

I've said it before: skiing is very much like a ballet. So, at times, is comprehending a child's thought process.

I was dressing a three-year-old skier for his first attempt at the sport. He was nervous about this new adventure.

"I want to ski with my big brother; he's on the green team," he said.

"Honey," I answered him, "I can't promise we'll be able to find the green team. They go pretty high up the mountain."

He calmly warned me of his forthcoming shortcoming and inability to stop it. "If I can't see my brother, I'll turn into a monster when I freak out."

I suspect he was speaking from experience.

She was the littlest of the little, so tiny, in fact, that our smallest ski boots are too big for her. I found this out at the most inconvenient of times: on the chairlift when her boot, still locked in the ski binding, slid off her foot. The boot and ski dangled below us. Thank goodness her skis were attached to each other with an "edgie-wedgie" that was holding the tips together. I struggled to reach the swinging ski, while still holding onto her so she too wouldn't slide off. It seemed to take forever, when it really only took a few seconds for her to giggle and wiggle her other foot free. I swear the skis were suspended in air for a nanosecond before I grabbed hold of one. We safely exited the chair, she in stocking feet and giggles, me holding her gear in one arm and her in the other. Good thing she was little.

While on the subject of chairlifts, here's my favorite kid story of the year:

As soon as the children are skilled enough to ski the upper mountain, I introduce chairlift safety into the lesson, beginning with the question, "What should you do if you accidentally don't get off the chairlift and start to go around the bullwheel?"

These are their typical answers: "Jump," "Ride back down," or "Start screaming!"

I tell them, "Well, first of all, don't jump because you could get hurt." Then I point to the stop gate. "Do you see that thing that looks like a fishing pole? That is called a stop gate. If you start to go around the wheel, kick it and the chairlift will stop. The attendant," I pointed at the guy in lift hut, "will come out and help you."

An astonished four-year-old snapped her head around to the attendant, then back to me and blurted, "He's real?"

I love to ski, I love to laugh, and I never minded a worthwhile challenge. That's why I love my job.

# *Walking with Children*

TEACHING PRESCHOOL-AGED CHILDREN THE FIERCELY FAST SPORT OF skiing has taught me how to walk in slow motion.

These small tots, many of whom have only been walking for a handful of months, are now walking in clunky ski boots. They have a tediously slow, often unsteady gait, but it is toward a new and wild adventure.

The path to that adventure begins with a walk across a bridge between the childcare center and the ski slope. Each child—without exception—stops to gaze into the water of the brook below. And what they see and what they wonder helps me to see and to wonder about things, too.

When I learned to walk slowly beside a child, a wondrous world I would have otherwise raced past was opened before me.

For instance, as the children look into the brook, their observations, like their personalities, are different.

The logical child says, "There are fish in there."

The inquisitive child asks, "Where are the frogs?"

The imaginative child wonders, "Is that where the bunnies wash their faces?"

The child after my own heart states, "I see a penguin!"

A child who sees a penguin where a penguin shouldn't be is the child who has not yet learned to be limited by the world's law of improbabilities. All things are possible until the boundaries of the world set up a wall around that child's imagination (and therefore probably his potential).

Penguins can be anywhere. The idea they can't live in Maine isn't entirely correct. The only reason penguins live where they do is because their predators don't have the gumption to live in freezing places (like Antarctica) or desertic or rocky regions (like the Galapagos Islands). (Doesn't knowing this give credence to the idea that your enemies are cowards at heart?)

It is entirely possible that penguins could live in Maine. Children instinctively know that penguins can go anywhere, do anything, and be anything...until the world convinces them otherwise.

Our days are bustling and busy—that is an absolute fact, but I urge you to occasionally walk slowly. Walk like a child, and perhaps you will see things or learn things you didn't think could be there.

# Child Speak

SOMETIMES, CHILDREN SPEAK IN A DIFFERENT LANGUAGE FROM ADULTS. They use the same words, but the meaning is masked in what I call child speak. Here are some examples I recently encountered while working at Sugarloaf's Perfect Turn Children's Ski School.

Once I squeezed onto the Moose Caboose (a sleigh pulled behind a snowmobile that carries us to the top of the beginner slope). As I settled my rear end beside a small child in the tiny (but only) space available, he aimed a mittened hand at me, squinted down the line of his thumb, and indignantly fired, "Psshhhh!"

I looked at him, a little indignant myself, and asked, "Did you just laser me?"

"That is a spider web," he educated me. "I am Spiderman."

I don't know the superheroes like I should, but I did recognize I was invading his personal space and he was trying to shoot me out of his way. I inched over to give him more room, but the child on the other side of me squeaked, "Ouch." I moved back.

"Sorry, Spidy," I said. "Put your web-shooters away; I'm stuck right here and no spider web can move me."

It's serious business, teaching five-year-olds how to ski. They have dreads and fears the adult world cannot possibly imagine. The way little children vocalize those fears is sometimes very creative.

"I don't want to pop them out right now to show you, but I have wings," one little guy confided to me.

"Are you an angel?" I asked.

"No," he said, and then continued, "I have wings with sharp points, and I don't have a button for them."

"Do you mean you can't control when they pop out?" I asked.

"Right," he said. "And if I go over a jump, they might pop out and I might fly away."

"As much as I'd like to see that, I guess we won't be going over any jumps," I reassured him.

"Right," he sighed in relief.

A daredevil and a doomsayer walked into a ski school...and went skiing with me. The daredevil went over a small jump and fell. He laid dramatically still, a crumpled mess of six-year-old and ski equipment.

The doomsayer turned to me and ominously proclaimed, "He's killed."

I don't claim to be an authority on the subject, nor do I always understand which emotions kids are trying to convey with their words, but I sure do love living close enough to their world that sometimes I'm lucky enough to hear their hearts.

We have nothing to fear but fear itself. (Tell that to a young child and watch how round their eyes can go!)

PART SEVEN

*"Writing is its own reward."*

—HENRY MILLER

## The Magic, the Power, the Love

MOST OF THE KIDS IN THE CHILDREN'S CENTER WERE PLAYING, WHICH IS a wonderful, vital thing to do, and children should play—a lot. But there were two children who sat by themselves, reading. I watched the little girl. Her eyes sparkled, no doubt because even though she sat quietly, her mind was anything but still. The twinkle in her eyes told me the words and pictures from the book were dancing in her mind.

All I could see of the little boy was the back of his head and the top of his book. He had told me earlier that he was reading the last volume in a series about dragons and the revenge of horned bunnies. He was so completely immersed in the story that he was oblivious to the boisterous, noisy play of others in the room.

That is the magic of books.

Earlier in the week I spoke to a college student who loves to read. She was telling me about writing a paper on the Aroostook War. The thing that surprises me most about Maine's Aroostook War is how few people I meet have heard about it (probably because not a shot was heard during it). But nevertheless it was indeed a war, a war over nearly one-third of northern Maine—a sizable piece of valuable timberland. Colonists were angry that our neighbors to the north and east were not only claiming the St. John River Valley as their own, but cutting the timber thereon. Hostilities between the two ensued. When Canada sent a thousand men to defend the claim, ten thousand indignant Americans showed up to answer, with another fifty thousand summoned to join them! Game over.

Learning new things is the power of books.

But the biggest reason my heart beats for books, the reason I feel excited when I set foot in a bookstore (especially an antique bookstore), is the absolute love of the images words can create. James

Russell Lowell, in his short story about a stagecoach ride to the north Maine woods in 1853, wrote about stopping at a tavern in the wee hours of the morning. His words: "A holster fumbled the door open and stood staring at, but not seeing us, with the sleep sticking out all over him."

The phrase "with the sleep sticking out all over him" painted such a vivid picture in my mind's eye that I had to stop looking at the book that held it. I put the volume down and stared into space to enjoy the art of that descriptive sentence.

I love that the writer allowed me to view a scene from over a hundred years ago. That's the beautiful thing about books: they let us experience other times, other people, other places.

We hold the world—the past, the present, and the future—in our hands when we hold books.

Our minds ferment in inactivity if we don't read. They become stagnant, airless rooms full of dust, cobwebs, and fog. Books open the doors and windows of the mind to allow everything out there in— ideas, images, thoughts, epiphanies, anger, fear, indignation, horror, humor, hate, disgust, convictions, lust, love, salvation.

Readers know this.

# Guns, Girls, Garments Gone Wrong, and Grandmothers with Blinders On

## Guns

I received a very late-night, unnerving text. It was a selfie of a man, a complete stranger to me; the message read: "I'll be there in a minute."

I texted him back. "If you are going to be here in a minute, you need to know I have a gun (several, actually), and I can shoot the eye out of a squirrel at a significant distance." I added, "And I bet your eye is bigger than a squirrel's."

He responded immediately, apologized profusely, explaining he had sent the text to a wrong number. I believe him, but just in case you find me missing, you'll find his photo on my cell phone.

## Girls and Garments Gone Wrong

When women get together, the conversation can turn to the strangest subjects. This particular day, because I had just experienced a humiliating incident of my skirt being tucked into my panties after exiting the ladies room, the conversation went to undergarment disasters.

My friends have all had mishaps and failures; it comes with the territory. I was telling them about the time my wraparound waitress skirt came unwrapped in front of customers and I had to back away from their table to keep my backside from ruining their appetite. A friend bested me when she told us about her last day at college, which was also her first date with the boy she had been eyeing all year. It was a brutally hot spring day, so she wore a sarong. At the end of the evening, she became undone when her garment did the same—it untied, slid down her body, and wrapped around her feet. She wasn't wearing a bra or underwear. Needless to say, that boy never called for a second date.

The daughter-in-law of a friend was trying to announce the

forthcoming birth of her second child at a family barbecue. When, after most of the day had passed and still nobody had paid attention, her disappointment became vocal. "Didn't anyone notice my son's T-shirt?"

All looked at the toddler's shirt. Bold letters across the chest read "Big Brother." My friend shrugged and told her daughter-in-law, "I noticed that but thought he was wearing a yard-sale find."

## Grandmothers with Blinders On

My daughter Kelly is the queen of deals. She's a shopper, but always for the bargain. She recently bought a stroller for her toddler on eBay. She told me she bought this one because a new one costs four hundred dollars, yet she got it for one hundred. Smart girl. I told her the second seat in this fancy-schmancy double stroller would be perfect for her son's baby bag or even for their small dog on long treks.

A few weeks later Kelly sent me a picture of her toddler in the newly arrived stroller; in the second seat was a chalkboard sign announcing another new arrival: "Baby girl arriving in January"

I'll forgive her for this blatant exposure of my naiveté, but only because she's having my first granddaughter.

# A Write Life

OCCASIONALLY, SOMEONE WILL ASK ME HOW THEY CAN BECOME A WRITER. "It's easy," I tell them. "Be born one."

Seriously, though, I can't answer their question. I can only speak for myself. I was indeed born a writer. It wasn't—still isn't—my own doing. My first hint came during elementary school. Remember putting your vocabulary words in sentences? Instead of writing, "The lion sat on a branch in a tree," I wrote, "The lion lounged on the tree branch, eyeing the herd, an evil desire tickling his heart." (Truly, I have the teacher's note to my mother.)

The second clue was during high school. I had always been an avid reader, but when asked to turn in a book report, I found it just as satisfying to make up my own story line, complete with characters and plot, and then turn in the subsequent fake-book book report.

A lot of people say they want to write so they can work from home. There are days I can't do that because there are too many other distractions that keep me from my keyboard—like the CD collection that needs to be alphabetized, or the pennies in the penny jar that need to be rolled, or the stack of papers on my desk that is begging to be restacked on the other side of the desk. So, I leave.

I used to think it grandstanding or boastful to work on a laptop at a trendy coffee shop. I thought those writers were trying to be seen, not write. Now I know differently. They go there because they too have silverware drawers that need reorganizing. Although there are coffee shops in my neighborhood, I choose to sit in the cafeteria of the local ski resort. The mountain looms in front of me in all its majestic glory. I watch ski patrol sweep down the slopes; their morning run coaxes the mountain awake. The scene nudges my creative juices, and they too begin to flow like a ballet.

As I sit slopeside, I find it too much of a coincidence that this morning's online thesaurus writing prompt is "nine words to help you navigate the slopes." I don't need words to help me navigate the slopes; I need strong knees, courage, and a modicum of skill. (I've also been told I need barrel arms. I don't like barrel arms.) Thank you, thesaurus, but today with a deadline looming I need words to navigate the page, not the slopes. Also, I need the courage to be an individual in both writing—and skiing—to keep my arms and my words lined up how I alone prefer them. Good writing is like skilled skiing—it takes practice and plain old-fashioned hard work to make a perfect turn or turn a perfect phrase.

I find the best path to fodder for writing is to keep my mouth closed but my ears and eyes forever open. Then I simply sit down and get to work. Easier said than done, because of course, there's that CD collection sitting on the self in utter alphabetical disarray.

Lastly, there is nothing overly special or pompous about writing (certainly not on my level, anyway). It's not like it's brain surgery (although it is). Writing is the same as every other success in life: you need hard work and determination to just do it. So, to those who ask about writing, I say, just do it.

# *Just (Didn't) Do It*

DON'T BOTHER TO READ THIS COLUMN; IT'S NOT ABOUT ANYTHING.

You see, as I begin to write this, February vacation has just ended. It's been a busy ten days at Sugarloaf Resort, where I am the ski coach for the childcare center. Now that vacation is over, everyone has left, leaving me feeling fulfilled and content, yet tired and unprepared to write anything anyone would be interested in reading.

I'd write about the past few days, but nobody wants to hear how long it took me to help a little boy turn his tears of fears into eyes full of wonderment upon seeing the chairlift ("airlift," he called it) and learning he can ride on that if he will ski down to it.

Neither is anyone interested in the little girl who, upon exiting that same chairlift for the first time, answered my question, "Well, what do you think?" with one of her own, "Do spiders sneeze?" (My days as a ski coach take a lot of interesting turns, as the thoughts of tiny tots veer here and there.)

She made me wonder, too. "I have no idea, but I'll find out," I told her. Although I detest, abhor, and really, really hate spiders and avoid any contact with them, I am interested in little things, so I spent my time not researching for my weekly newspaper column, but looking up spider anatomy. Yes, I googled it, and no, they don't have noses, so, no, they can't sneeze, but they can smell through receptors on their legs. No matter how slim the odds are that I will ever be asked that question again, I'll have an answer. It's all about being prepared, you see. However, all that preparedness left me unprepared to meet this week's deadline.

And of course, guests at my B&B kept me busy. They shared their stories with me over breakfast, but none made it to paper in time.

Then, my skis disappeared. Nearly everyone told me my skis must have blown into the brook that runs alongside the slope where I put them. It seemed a little far-fetched that both skis would wash away in the water, but after three days of searching, I started to believe they had. Then, just as mysteriously as they vanished, they reappeared; I found them leaning against the fence near where I'd left them. There went three days spent searching, not researching.

My plan was to get straight to work. Except it snowed. The mountain had a lot of powder; I have a lot of ski buddies, a free pass, and skis again. (It's true what they say about life in the mountains being tough—tough for you if you can't live here.)

The next day, just as I headed off to a quiet spot to write the fascinating story about the city of Portland burning to the ground four times in its history, a friend called. "Meet me at The Bag!" I can never turn down a Bag lunch. Then of course we had to go to the gym to work off our indulgences and then to the hot tub to ease that pain. The only story being written after all that was that night, in the form of my deep-sleep dreams.

I apologize to the readers for not writing a worthy column this week; I just didn't do it.

# *Birds on a Wire*

THE DOVES ARE PERCHED RANDOMLY ACROSS THE ELECTRIC WIRES outside my window. They look very much like musical notes on a sheet of staff paper. But these musical characters are silent as they set themselves against the very early morning chill. If I had a piano and the talent, I'd play their song, but my only keyboard is this one, so I fall miserably short and describe it.

## *Lacuna*

I AM COMPLETELY AND UTTERLY ANNOYED WITH THE ENGLISH LANGUAGE. Although some words are redeeming—like *lacuna*. Definition: a blank space or a missing part; gap. Let me use it in a sentence: The story I'm working on is nothing but incondite words separated by abysmal lacunas.

*Lacuna* also defines my memory...and my good intentions... and my checkbook.

# *I Count*

I STOOD ON MY PORCH (STILL IN MY JAMMIES) AND RAISED A CUP OF COFFEE with my very lazy arm at the marathon runners as they jogged by.

I tried to pick out the ones who are my bed and breakfast guests, but I can't. Neither can I count their numbers, so I count the ones who lean way forward when they run: fifteen.

And I count the ones who swing their arms high, threatening to punch themselves in the chin: four.

I tried to count the ones who couldn't possibly make it to the end. Only one of those for sure: me

I may not be able to run a twenty-six-mile marathon, but still, I count.

# *Provocation*

I COLLECT ANTIQUE MAINE BOOKS—PREFERABLY THOSE EDITIONS published before 1900—and preferably nonfiction books with a historical theme, but I'll read anything (if I can get past the first paragraph). My fondness for old books began when my grandmother gave me her copy of *Canoe and Camera: Two Hundred Miles Through the Maine Forests,* published in 1880.

Last evening, tucked in with tea and comforter, I sat by the fireplace in my library and read a short story titled "A Dead Letter" from another one of her books, *Along New England Roads* (Harper & Brothers, 1892). The story is a mystery, and it immediately caught my mind and reeled me in. It had all the right ingredients to make it a delicious tale: good writing, beautifully descriptive woodland settings, interesting and identifiable characters—all the stuff that generates the desire to know where would I end up on this literary adventure: enlightened, entertained, amused? All of those things?

This story was so completely captivating that it picked me up and carried me across the pages, almost against my will like any good story does. (It's a mystery in itself how a writer can grab us and move us forward on a road built merely of words.)

I read and sipped and sighed, completely delighted and content to have a few quiet moments to enjoy a story, the thoughts from the mind and pen of another, from another time, made available to me across the generations in the form of the written word.

And then several pages later the story ended abruptly without solving the mystery. It stopped without satisfying my curiosity. It didn't even have the common decency to explain its point. "A Dead Letter" dead-ended. It was like an episode of *The Twilight Zone.* There wasn't a payoff for taking the time to open the book and turn the pages.

What a horrible thing to do to a reader. A reader should be able to trust that a story will finish, not just end. A reader should feel well fed; I did not, but it wasn't my stomach that growled.

The story ending infuriated me and I thought, "What the heck?"

## *The Beautiful*

The beautiful are beautiful
Because they smile freely,
Laugh often,
Love without reserve,
And embrace the world and those in it with wild abandon.

# The Stories

YOU'VE HEARD IT SAID: "EVERYONE HAS A STORY." I THINK EVERYONE IS a story. If Shakespeare was right and all the world is a stage, all the men and women merely players, then our lives are the stories that play out upon it. The choices we make in life coupled with our experiences—both those we enjoy and those we merely survive, the things we witness, the people with whom we interact—are the ingredients of the ink. How all this molds us or changes us is the author. We are the story. The life that is a story is built on moments that make the words, months that form the sentences, and years that build the chapters.

Think of all the lives that have been, all the lives that are now, and the lives that will be. Think of each and every one of them individually—you can't because the number is mind-boggling. But still, you have an opportunity each day of your life to be an influence on hundreds if not thousands. How many life stories have you impacted and in what manner?

You are a word, a sentence, or a paragraph that is or will be a part of someone's life story. What sort of word are you? Are you an ugly word like *mulligrubs* or *unctuous*? Or are you a beautiful word like *billet-doux*—a love letter?

What sort of paragraph do you form in another's life? Do you make it into the chapter category, or do you peter out somewhere near the beginning? Does your part end in a steadfast period, an exhilarating exclamation point, or an unreliable question mark? Which stories are outstanding because you had a hand in writing them?

I recently noticed a very strange and scary man who seemed to be touched. I wondered what experience or what sort of person touched him to make him like that. Then I remembered he too is a story and because he's so unusual, I bet his story is fascinating. I recognize no matter how weird he is, he is priceless because his story is unlike anyone else's. That makes him more valuable than every other person—no matter which line he reaches on the world's measuring stick. The same can be said for you and me. Because our experiences are unique to us alone, we are unique and valuable.

We don't know the end of the story until the end has come, but we know every story—boring or brilliant—is worth the read, worthy of print, worthy of being more than just a footnote.

Here is the beautiful part of this story: every morning, every new day, is a chance to be a beautiful word, powerful paragraph, or stunning chapter in someone's life.

# The Word of the Day

The day becomes procellous
When others grow jealous.
(They think I'm word zealous.)
I confess to solecism,
Using big wordism,
But deny gasconade.
It's just the e-mailed word of the day,
Forgotten when I walk away.

# *Working Through a Dry Spell*

I⟋T WAS BOUND TO HAPPEN. I GOT WRITER'S BLOCK. MY SUMMER WAS incredibly busy, meaning my mind was one of two things: so full that it seized up, or so empty that the only thing between my ears was a hollowed-out cave. I sought advice from real writers, hoping to find a cure, and was told to try these tricks, one each day.

Day 1: Write every single day.
Okay, I will write every day. That's enough for today.

Day 2: Set deadlines and keep them.

Dear Editor,
When you said my deadline is today, did you mean today today or tonight today?
How about tomorrow?

Day 3: Examine any deep-seated issues.
I checked the depth of the recliner in the living room. Yup, it's deep and soft and lovely and inviting, and I think that's where I need to be. Right now.

Day 4: Write about anything.
I ate a pineapple. It tasted like a pineapple. This idea is about as dumb as a pineapple.

Day 5: Read a book written by an author you admire.
From *Blue Highways: A Journey into America* by William Least Heat-Moon: "When the Plains Indians realized their fate and freedom were in the hands of the conquering white man, they donned cloth shirts that they believed rendered them indestructible and danced for the return of warriors, bison and their old ways." The author, describing

the 1890s ghost dances and the *dying rattles of a people*, wrote: "Their last defense was delusion."

Their last defense was delusion.

After reading that line, it occurred to me I would never conquer the art of great writing like this author had. I would never gain such a talent to perfectly match words—words that play over and over in the mind of a reader—like his words played in mine.

I felt as dry as an old bone and yearned for the days of free-flowing ideas, muses without end, and fingers that danced on the keys to keep up.

But writer's block hadn't yet defeated me; that wasn't possible. I had more to say! I decided if I put on my iPod and danced, inspiration would come.


Day 6: Get out of the house and go shopping.

I knew as soon as I arrived I would love it. The handful of dried-up, windblown leaves and a solitary feather lying on the stairs just inside the entrance gave it away. They—like me—had blown in through the open door. The fragile leaves and that one downy feather were at the end of their journey, yet they spoke volumes: the used-book store I was visiting was not presumptuous; it was a little bit messy.

Castoffs were welcome there.

"I love this place," I said to no one.

Unlike the leaves and feather, I continued down the steps and entered a small room filled to the rafters with the aroma of antiquity and age and musty wisdom and books and the absolute joy of discovering their stories. Like discovering those castoffs of wild things at the door, I just knew I would discover inspiration if I entered. Wrapped in the scent of years gone by were stack upon stack of bounded treasures. Rich in fullness, they lay on shelves and in piles on chairs and benches and in every available space, waiting for me to peer into their souls simply by opening their jackets. Wonderful books with titles such as *Songs with Tears* and *Don't Slip in the Mustard.*

I had just picked up a copy of the book *Letters of E.B. White* when my friend called from the top of the stairs, "It's time to go!"

"But," I protested, unable to lift my head from the sheets, "E.B. White wrote a letter and it's to me!"

"We really need to go now!" she insisted.

"Fine, fine," I gave in. "It's time I went home anyway. I feel like writing."

# I Like Books

I HAVE A BOOKMARK SOMEWHERE THAT READS, "I'M NEVER LONELY; I have a book." I'm not sure where that bookmark is because I read about ten books at a time. I move in between books like a judge moves between the tables at a middle-school science fair—sampling and savoring each experiment. For me, books are experiments of thought.

For a long time I couldn't read when I wrote because I started to write like the writer I was reading. I think reading ten or so books at a time helped me with that absorption problem. My words are no longer the feat of another's passage; they have merged and mixed, blended with my experiences to become mine.

Reading only one book is like buying in bulk at the big-box store, but being allowed to eat only one thing at a time—as if I had to consume five pounds of meatballs before opening the ten-pound can of spaghetti sauce and three-pound bag of pasta, and then finish those before I could eat the gigantic bag of pistachios. I never minded if my food touched or overlapped; I actually prefer it. It's tastier that way.

There is a hitch: when reading so many books at once, I soak up different things from each, and all the random thoughts and ideas, stories and characters meld into one great big theatrical drama that takes on a life of its own and plays out in my mind. Although it thoroughly entertains me, it becomes a point of embarrassment when I try to recommend a book to another. Sometimes I cannot say who wrote which or where I read what.

As a young mother, I was an undisciplined reader. When I picked up a book, I couldn't put it down until it was finished. My mind was full, but my cupboards were empty, my home was in shambles, and my children looked like dirty little ignorant things. So, I started reading to them and found my world—and the lives my kids—all the richer for it.

One of the things I love about reading books is the potential for surprise. You never know what the next sentence or paragraph holds. All of a sudden, there it is: a new thought, a peek around the corner at an old idea, perhaps a revelation, a revolution, repulsion, or conviction. The words jump out and grab hold of your mind, and because you read them, they are now part of you and can never leave. And those words, that sentence, or those paragraphs can completely change your mood, your day, your evening, or the way you perceive something for the rest of your life.

# *Thankful*

I WAS SITTING AT MY KITCHEN TABLE ONE VERY EARLY MORNING, FINISHING off a slice of chocolate chip zucchini bread as I began to write my newspaper column which are non-fiction essays on Maine life. This column would appear in the paper that came out during Thanksgiving week, so I wanted it to be timely. Instead of concentrating on that, I was wishing I had another piece of bread, not because I was still hungry, but because it was delicious and I simply wanted more. So there I sat with a blank word-processor page and an empty breakfast plate in front of me. No thought or idea stood out for me to grasp and turn into words. The only thing standing out that drab morning was the title of the Thanksgiving piece, "Thankful," and it did so in a bold cranberry-colored font.

That was as far as I could get, so I stared out the window at another cranberry—Cranberry Peak (only it was blue in the day's breaking light). A cloud of smoke from a chimney hovered over the top of a bare-limbed tree, which wore the thick white cloud like a bad toupee. But it was the trees on Cranberry Peak that had my attention; they were devoid of their leaves (like my mind was devoid of any words for my column). Again I turned my attention to writing, but all I could think about was the blank page, the empty plate, the barren trees, and wordless me. Blank, empty, barren, and less-ness—these were the things that seemed to surround me. It is an easy trap to fall into, dwelling on the missing things, the loss and the emptiness that can surround us at times. It wouldn't take much effort to get into the bad habit of waking up every day and seeing life that way.

I stared at my page and that cranberry-colored word staring back at me: *Thankful.* Thankful for a blank page? Yes, for it is an opportunity for innumerable pieces of art in the form of words and ideas, thoughts and inspiration.

I was thankful for the barren mountain out there. Imagine the unobstructed view of what lies ahead when one climbs to the top.

With all those dead leaves (those bygone things) out of the way, a clearer viewpoint emerges—perhaps even an exsighting view of one's destination or destiny!

I realized I should be thankful for a plate of crumbs as well, because it meant I had a full belly. I glanced at my plate. There was a smidgen of chocolate left from my slice of chocolate chip zucchini bread. I wiped it up with a fingertip and licked off that last tiny bit of yum. Yes, I was thankful, for even a micro amount of chocolate is still a taste of chocolate.

We have so much more than most, even when it seems like we have nothing. If I practice thankfulness in everything, I will come to understand that.